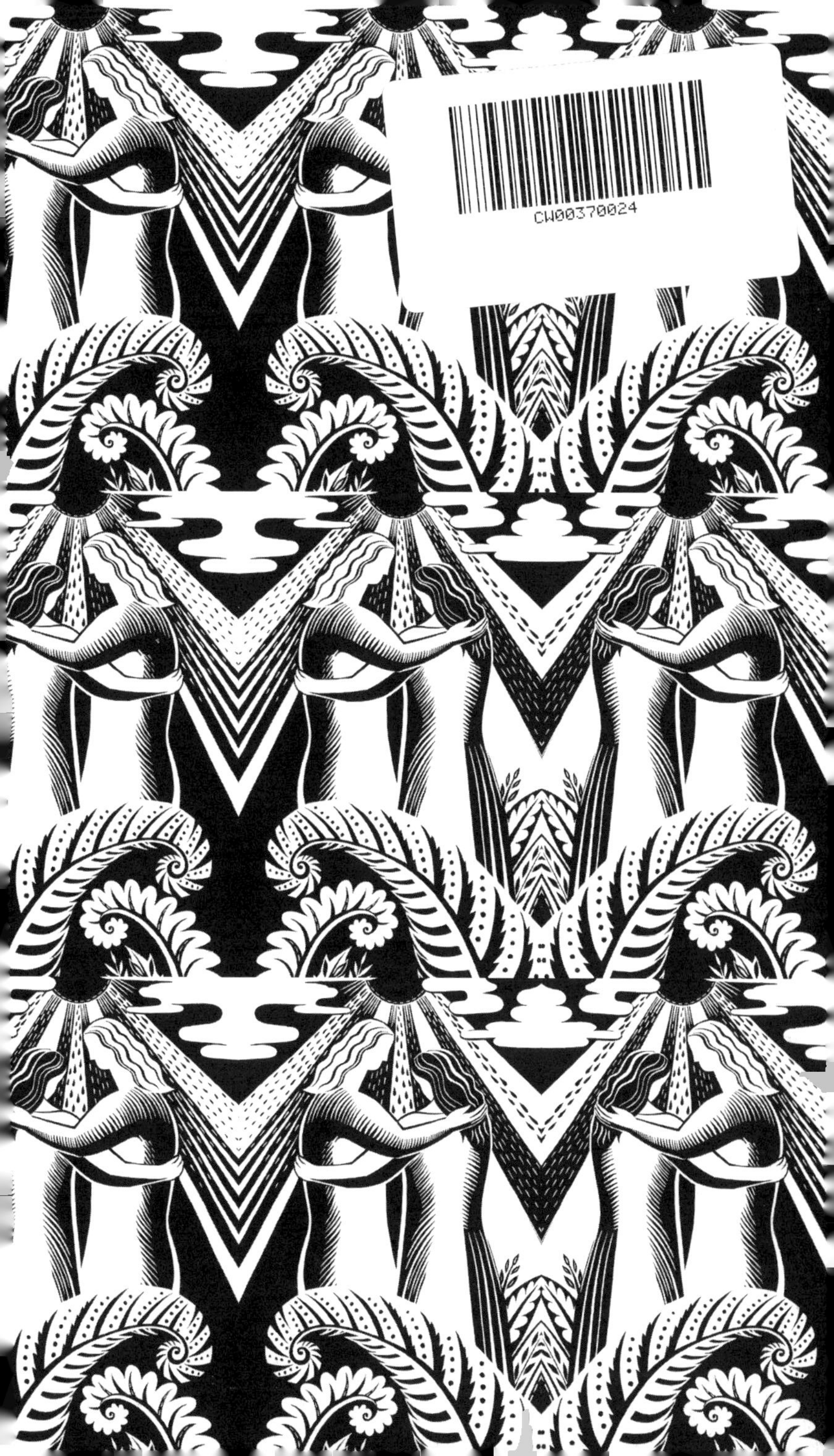

Mindfulness and
Compassion

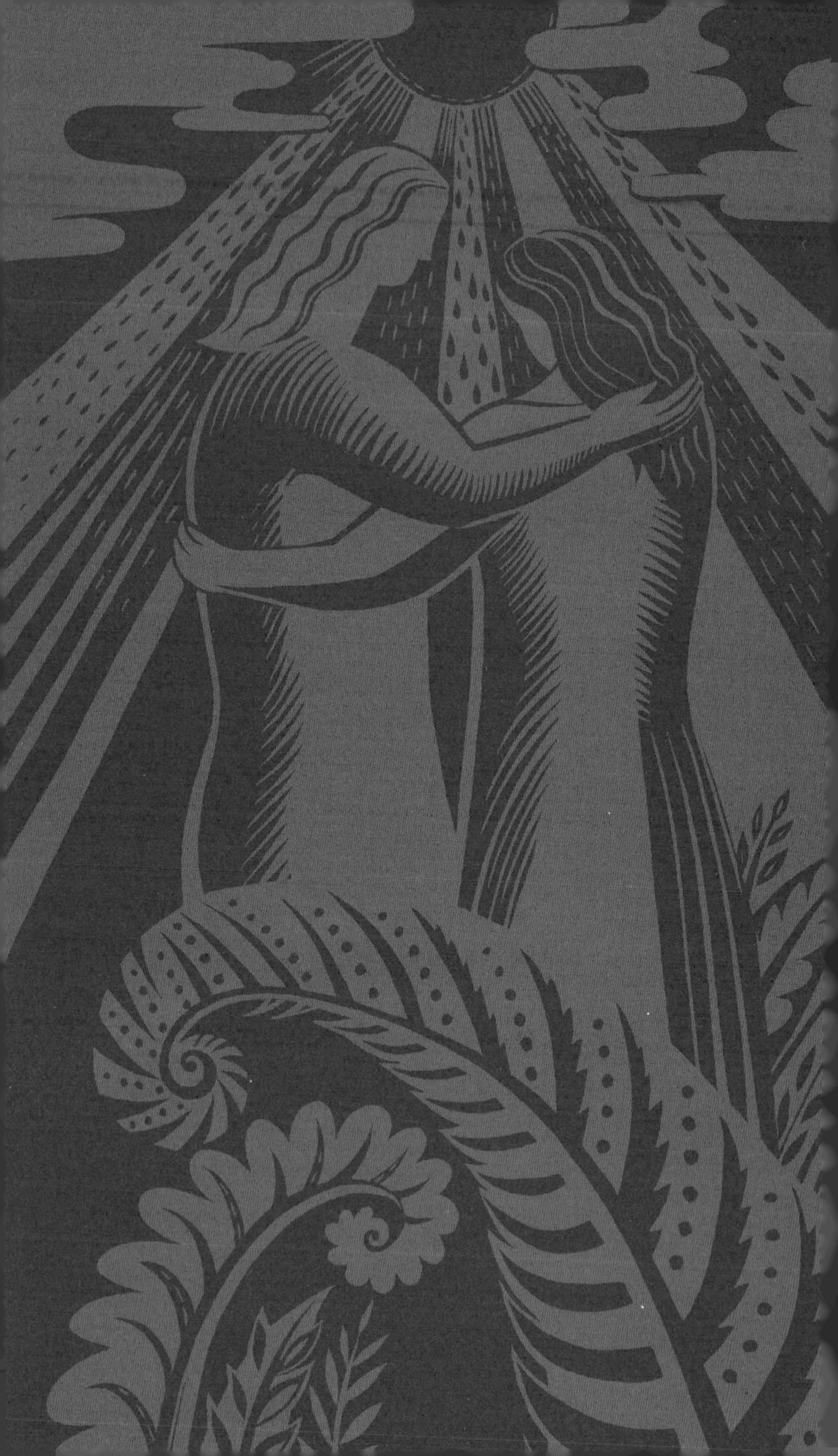

Mindfulness and Compassion

Embracing Life with Loving-Kindness

The Happy Buddha

Leaping Hare Press

First published in the UK in 2015 by

Leaping Hare Press

210 High Street, Lewes
East Sussex BN7 2NS, UK
www.leapingharepress.co.uk

Text copyright © Suryacitta 2015
Design and layout copyright © The Ivy Press Limited 2015

British Library Cataloguing-in-Publication Data
A catalogue record for this book is available from
the British Library

ISBN: 978-1-78240-288-6

This book was conceived, designed and produced by

Leaping Hare Press

Creative Director PETER BRIDGEWATER
Publisher SUSAN KELLY
Commissioning Editor MONICA PERDONI
Art Director WAYNE BLADES
Editorial Director TOM KITCH
Project Editor JAYNE ANSELL
Editor JENNI DAVIS
Designer GINNY ZEAL
Illustrator SARAH YOUNG

Printed in China
Colour origination by Ivy Press Reprographics

Distributed worldwide (except North America) by
Thames & Hudson Ltd., 181A High Holborn,
London WC1V 7QX, United Kingdom

1 3 5 7 9 10 8 6 4 2

CONTENTS

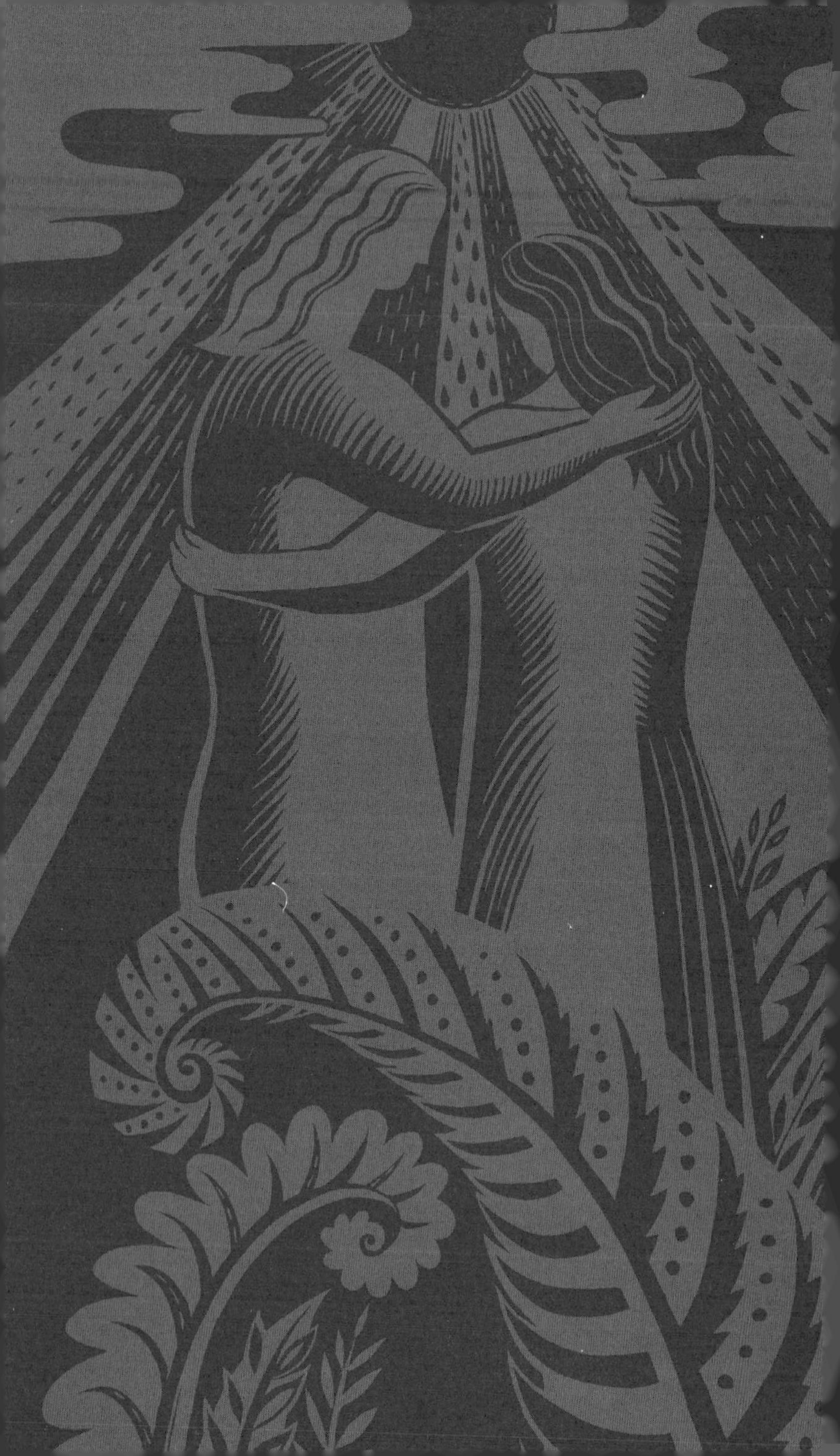

INTRODUCTION

*The essence of mindfulness is always compassion
and compassion is about relating. We are always in
relationship to something, somebody. Right now you
are in relationship to these words, to the chair you are
sitting on. At other times you are in relationship to
your own thoughts and feelings; often these can be
painful. In other moments, you are in relationship
to other people – family, friends, work colleagues
and even strangers. It is the quality of our
relationships that determines the
quality of our lives.*

COMPASSIONATE LIVING

◆

There is a saying in the mindfulness tradition – how we relate to one thing is how we relate to everything. When we are compassionate towards ourselves, with sympathy for our own shortcomings and pain, we cannot be anything else to other people. Compassion is naturally 'other-regarding'.

COMPASSION HAS NOT ONLY A SOFT, tender side but also strength and power. True compassion takes everything into account, including ourselves. It is not about running around helping others, and running around helping others does not necessarily come from compassion – often the motivation is *people-pleasing* and wanting to be liked, or feeling a sense of responsibility. It is not about always being there to get people out of trouble, but knowing that sometimes the best thing is to let them find their own way – often this is how we grow. A good mother, for example, allows her baby to get off its knees and learn to walk. This process involves the baby falling, which can be painful for the mother to see – but a wise mother knows that the falling is a part of growing and will help the baby eventually to walk.

It is necessary to understand that although we talk about practising and developing compassion, that is not how it really works. To say 'I am more compassionate than you' shows you have completely missed the point. Why? Because compassion is not a personal possession. Compassion arises when the *self* or the *me* is no longer concerned with how it appears to the world. So a true compassionate act is not done for glory. It is done – and that is it. It is done to alleviate the pain and suffering of either ourselves or others, including animals.

Opening to the Sun of Compassion

Compassion is like the sun. We do not need to create the sun; we simply wait until the clouds part and the sun will shine. The self is like the clouds – all our practice, whether we know it or not, is about thinning the clouds of self-interest so that the sun of compassion can shine on all.

However, learning to relate to our own and other people's pain in each moment is where it all begins. One of the key messages of this book is to learn to turn toward your own pain, your own shortcomings, without criticism and conflict; you will then start the process of thinning out the clouds of your own self-interest and opening to the sun of compassion and happiness.

It is lack of love for ourselves that inhibits
our compassion toward others. If we make friends
with ourselves, then there is no obstacle to opening
our hearts and minds to others.

ANON

EXERCISE

COMPASSION MEDITATION

Preparing to Meditate

• Read through each meditation a few times before you begin.

• Take up your meditation posture: find a comfortable upright chair and sit relaxed and alert, feeling your contact with the floor and with the chair.

• If you wish, set a meditation timer. There are plenty available online and using one allows you just to relax into the meditation without thinking about the time.

Compassion meditation, also known as 'loving-kindness', stems from the Buddhist tradition and is becoming increasingly popular; a lot of research has been carried out into the benefits of regular practice. This meditation takes us through five stages of practice: compassion for self; compassion for a good friend or someone we like; compassion for a neutral person with whom we have a little contact but are not intimately connected; compassion for a person whom we find difficult; compassion for all beings.

Take up your meditation posture. Feel your breath for a few minutes. When you feel ready, take your attention to your heart area (middle of the chest) and notice how it feels there. Be honest. Whether you find sadness, happiness, a heavy kind of feeling or virtually nothing, acknowledge it and gently stay with it. Bring your self to mind as you sit and just rest with that sense of yourself for a few moments. You are now ready to move into the five stages of the loving-kindness practice. Do each stage for three to four minutes, then come back to your breath for a minute or two.

1. While staying in your heart area, drop in the phrase, 'May I be happy, may I be well.' Notice any responses you have to these words. If you find yourself drifting, then gently and kindly bring yourself back to the present and go back to your heart area. Remember, this is a loving-kindness meditation, and we develop compassion by how we are toward ourselves, so notice if you are critical of yourself, and if you are, let the thoughts go and gently come back to your heart area. After a minute or two, drop in the phrase again and rest in the heart. Nothing needs to happen here; we are not looking for a big explosive cosmic love feeling. It is more like planting seeds of loving-kindness that will grow over time. After three to four minutes, come back to the breath.

2. When it feels right, bring to mind a good friend and wish them well in the same way – 'May you be happy, may you be well.' Again, gently stay in the heart area and be honest about what is there. There may be feelings of warmth, or you may feel pretty neutral or even have feelings of ill will toward your friend. Be absolutely honest about how you feel toward them; honesty also includes not being sure. Sometimes we see that

our feelings toward our good friend are mixed, or we realize that we are a little resentful of something they said. All this is absolutely fine and is part of the practice. If you do find warmth and good feelings toward them, then enjoy them and allow them to grow. Do not force any feelings out of awareness and do not try to bring feelings into it. What is happening should be happening because it *is* happening. After a minute or two, drop in the words again. After three to four minutes, allow your friend to stand to one side in your imagination and come back to the breath.

3. Bring to mind a neutral person. This is maybe the post person, or a local shopkeeper. It is someone who you see about but don't have a relationship with. Start in the same way as previous stages, then drop in the phrase once again, and be honest, it is the key. No matter how you feel toward them, it is OK. You may feel very little but that is fine. It may be worth reflecting that this person wants to be happy, just like you. They have fears, they have wishes for a good life, as you do. They have people they love and people they find difficult in their life. After three to four minutes, allow this person to stand to one side and come back to the breath.

4. When you feel ready, bring to mind a difficult person – maybe a long-time difficult person, or somebody you are having difficulty with at present. Repeat the practice of the previous stages, then when the time is up, allow the difficult person to stand aside and come back to the breath.

5. In the final stage, bring together in your mind all four people from the previous stages. Wish all four people well. Don't worry about getting it right. You don't need vivid pictures in your mind or to feel each person's presence, it is the intention that matters. Then include in your awareness all living beings, in an ever-increasing circle. You may casually bring to mind all neighbours in your street or village. Then move out to wish happiness to all people in your country. Again, it doesn't matter how you do this; you are certainly not trying to visualize everyone, which would give you quite a headache. It's more about having a sense of people. Then, in your own way, bring other nations to mind. We all just want to be happy. Remember, you don't need to feel something special here; honesty and staying with how you feel is what is important. You can also bring to mind all animals, as they wish to be free from suffering too, it seems. After a few minutes of this, you can end and spend a few minutes with yourself.

Coming back to the breath allows us to give ourselves space to see what is happening in the bigger picture. For example, we may find that we have been tense while practising. This allows us to see how we may be trying to achieve something or trying to make something happen in the practice.

So be compassionate toward yourself here. It's ironic that often we approach the 'kindness' practice with very little kindness, often judging ourselves for falling short of how we think we should be practising.

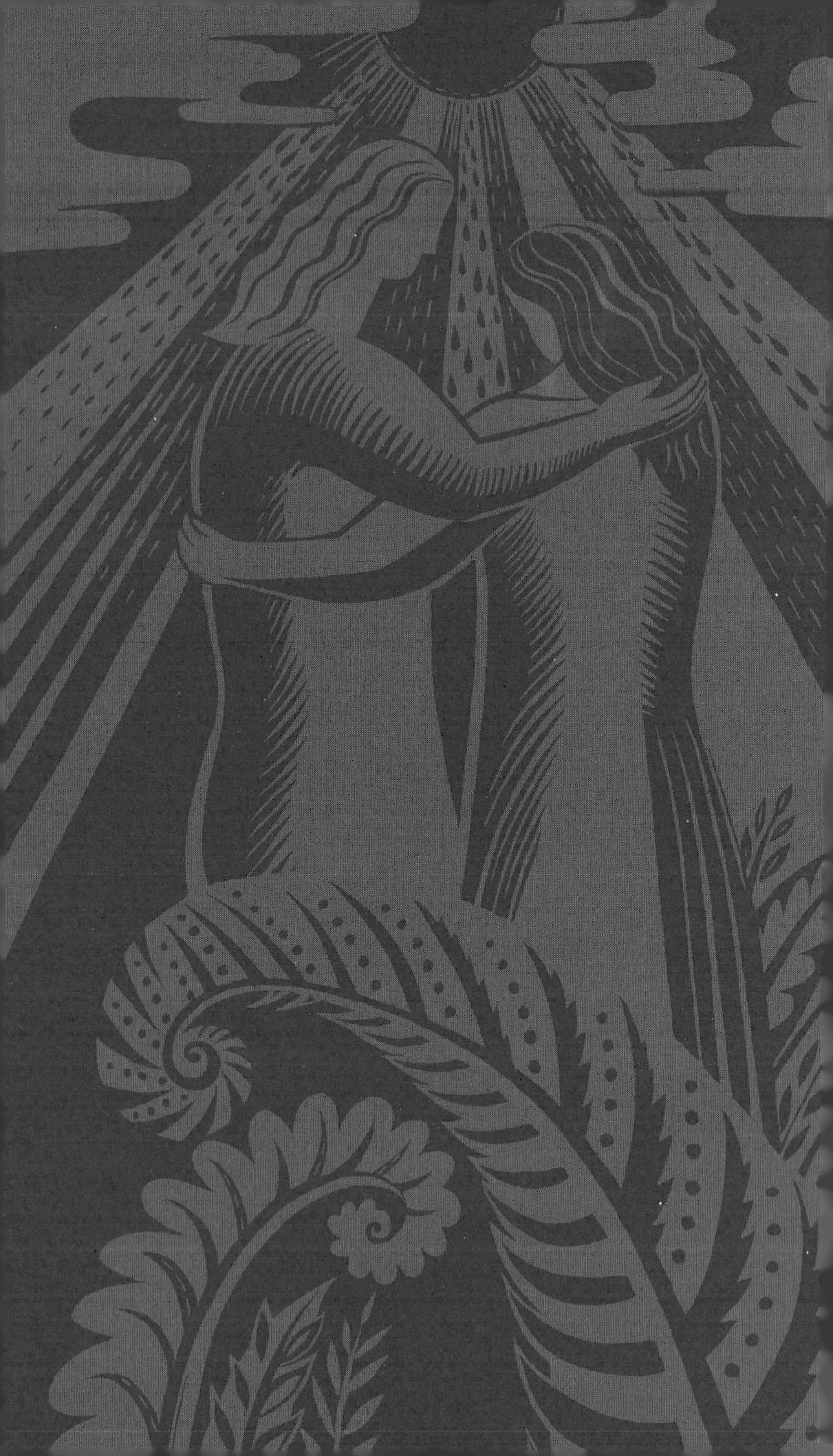

CHAPTER ONE

MINDFULNESS

*Imagine a large block of ice. Inside is
a jewel, a beautiful, sparkling, glittering jewel.
We cannot always see it, but we know it is there.
We have felt it, seen it, been taken to moments of joy
by it. It has always existed and always will. No matter
where it is, no matter how hidden, it always remains
a jewel. Even if it's coated with dust and grime by
decades of neglect, all it needs is a little attention to
sparkle again, for it is the jewel of a joyful life –
a life lived in mindfulness.*

THE JEWEL IN THE ICE

◆

The jewel of joy is our birthright. We may sense it inside ourselves and wonder how we can enjoy its presence more than we do – yet how can we experience it when life seems beset with problems? How can we replace our angst and confusion with ease and clarity?

IT MAY SEEM TO us that *our* life is not blessed with the jewel of joy. It may seem that it doesn't exist at all – that it is just a fairytale. The clue to why we may not experience the jewel fully lies in the fact that it is embedded in the block of ice. We could think of the ice as our resistance to how life is in any moment. It is made up of our rigid views and judgements that life should be a certain way, free from pain. For example, when somebody criticizes us, we have a tendency to dwell on what they said and blame them for how we feel. This is one way we build up the layers of ice. In this scenario, we are reluctant to experience our own hurt. But the moment we let go of our blaming thoughts and instead tend with compassion to the feeling of hurt, the ice begins to melt. The mindful and compassionate experiencing of sorrow itself melts the ice. Of course, we may also decide to say something to that person, but if we are willing to work with our anger, then what we say will be much more considered.

Another way we build up the block of ice is by trying to keep away any painful feelings from the past; but a joyful life does not mean we never experience pain. Paradoxically, pain is a facet of the jewel. We try desperately to deny it by trying to make it go away or by taking it personally, but we only create suffering. For example, we may feel sad about something that has happened to us, but because we feel uncomfortable about feeling sad, we 'freeze' out that experience. I have met many people in my work as a mindfulness teacher who think that feeling sadness (or any other difficult emotion) is bad, for whatever reason. If they feel sad, it means that there is something wrong with them or their life. However, sadness is a natural human emotion and it is there to be experienced. If we don't learn to turn toward our emotions with mindfulness and kindness, we will continue to distance ourselves from the jewel and experience only the ice.

Sadness is a natural human emotion and is there to be experienced

Melting the Ice

If we put ice in the sun, it will melt, and whatever is hidden within it will, at some point, be revealed. This is similar to the process we must engage in to experience the jewel of joy more fully in our lives, and it is what mindfulness is all about. Mindfulness is like the sun – it melts and heals what it shines upon. As we melt the ice, it reverts to its original nature – flowing water. In a similar way, as we melt the ice of our

un-experienced emotions, those very emotions begin to flow again. And as the ice continues to melt, we begin to sense more aliveness and energy.

So to melt the ice and allow the jewel to bring you more joy, notice the rigid views that you cling to. Views like 'I don't want this to be happening'; 'Life shouldn't be like this'; 'My life will never be the same again.' Learn to let them go and come into the present moment, which is simple and never complicated. Turn toward your experience as it is – hearing, tasting, smelling, seeing and feeling – without your mental and emotional overlay, and you will slowly melt the ice that keeps you from living a joyful and fulfilling life.

We can see the rest of this book, and indeed the rest of our lives, as the process of melting the ice. Sensing the jewel in the first place is the easy part; the challenge is to melt the ice that surrounds it. This is our work and this is what I aim to share with you.

We always work with the ice with compassion – a very important aspect of mindfulness.

MINDFULNESS MEDITATION
& HOW TO DO IT

◆

Mindfulness meditation is not about having wonderful experiences and feeling cosmic bliss. It's not about having a blank mind and developing strange psychic powers. It isn't even about self-improvement, a very common misperception. Meditation is about the person who is meditating. It is about you – all of you.

A FEW YEARS AGO, my partner and I decided we wanted to start growing our own vegetables, so we took on an allotment. It was very close to our home and we were very excited about our first visit. When we got there, we were a little surprised to find it was waist-high in weeds. There wasn't a weed-free patch to be seen. We decided to get it turned over by a friend who had a digger and it looked great – not a weed in sight. We then laid old carpet on the soil so the weeds wouldn't come back.

However, a few weeks later, I pulled back a section of the carpet so we could plant vegetables, and saw that the weeds had started to grow back again. I was amazed! I thought we had got rid of them, or at least some of them. But all we had succeeded in doing was to contain them for a while – they were still there, beneath the carpet, just waiting to ruin our vegetable patch.

It made me realize that we would never be rid of the weeds if we just covered them with carpet. To be completely free of them,

we had to get them at the root and this was much harder work; but once we got them by the root – which meant digging with spades and using our hands – we could then use some of them as compost to grow good vegetables in the future.

Covering the weeds with carpet and hoping they will disappear is the lazy way, and this is often how we approach meditation – the lazy way. We experience our 'mind weeds' as agitation, worry, anxiety and restlessness, and most of us come to meditation thinking that it will rid us of them. We don't want to do the hard work of uprooting them – we just want to throw a carpet over them and be done with it; but as we can see from my experience at the allotment, this doesn't work. It may appear to be working, for a while; but sooner or later, those mind weeds are going to spring back to life. It is when this happens that people stop meditating – 'It doesn't work,' they say. And it won't – unless we start 'digging and getting our hands dirty'. By this, I don't mean analysis or trying to work out why we are the way we are; it is simpler than that. I mean we must be willing to face our experience in the moment.

A willingness to embrace and work with
what is lies at the core of all meditation practice.[1]

FROM 'WHEREVER YOU GO, THERE YOU ARE'
JON KABAT-ZINN

Working with Our Mind Weeds

So how exactly *do* we work with our mind weeds? How does meditation help us? Anybody nowadays can just pick up a book or a CD and begin meditation and it may help them lead better lives if they practise well. But to get the most out of meditation, we need to know the subtleties of it, to understand what it really is, rather than what we think it is. Most of us think it is about relaxing, because relaxed is what we want to be. It's not that meditation is *not* about relaxing – but this is only a very small part of it. If we use meditation as a technique to relax, when we stop using the technique we will be stressed again. This is because the mind weeds – the cause of our stress and agitation – are still present.

If we use meditation solely as a tool to relax, we will in all likelihood be disappointed. Meditation helps us relax, but not through *trying* to relax. Let me explain. We come to meditation with a certain amount of agitation and restlessness. Our minds are busy and our bodies are tense – rigid, like the ice I spoke of earlier. Mindfulness is learning how to relax into our agitation and distress; it is about learning how to melt the ice of our resistance, and this can only be done with a compassionate attitude. We hope that meditation will work and if we approach it right it will make a difference – but it is *how* we approach it that is crucial.

When most people begin meditation, they want to rid themselves of any bad feelings and negative thoughts. This,

EXERCISE

MINDFULNESS OF BREATHING

The Mindfulness of Breathing is practised all over the world and has been for many centuries. If you only do one practice from this book, I suggest this to be the one. Practise this meditation for around 10–15 minutes.

- To begin, take up your meditation posture (see p.10).
- Start with your eyes open and rest your gaze on the floor in front. If your eyes want to close after a while, allow them to. Before we take our attention to our breath, it is good to establish a connection with the body. So spend a minute sensing into the body before moving to the breath. Notice the shape of your body; feel the weight of your body sitting in the chair.
- Now take your attention to the chest and belly area and become aware of the movement there as you breathe. Just feel the movement.
- If you notice you are lost in thinking, that's fine; let the thoughts drift away and then return to the body and breath. Relax, because there is no doing this wrong. If there are any external sounds, just let them be.
- Notice the cycle of the breath – the rising and the falling. Notice how the breath feels – long and smooth, short and shallow; just notice. You are not trying to breathe in a special way, just as it comes.
- There is no need for judgements or opinions here – if you have them, just let them drift away like clouds in the sky. Return to your body and breath … body and breath … body and breath.
- Keep it simple … You are not looking for anything special to happen.
- When you are ready to bring the session to a close, simply open your eyes and then sit as you wish. Feel yourself in the chair once again. Take a few moments to absorb what you have done.

of course, is understandable. But we don't get rid of them by going to war with them; this only creates a tension. There is a part of us that is trying to get rid of another part, and this attitude actually creates the ice rather than melts it. We need to use a different way, and that is to be compassionate *toward* that which is causing us pain. This is often the last thing we want to do, but moving toward that difficulty is what heals it.

TRAINING THE PUPPY MIND

Anyone who engages in mindfulness practice knows that an agitated mind is an unhappy mind. Our minds can be likened to a puppy. Puppies are rarely still, and they wander; it is in their nature. But puppies need to be trained, for their sakes and ours. Our minds are similar.

HAVE YOU EVER TRIED TO TRAIN A PUPPY? My dog, Jaya, is two years old at the time of writing and we got him when he was eight weeks old. He was gorgeous and he was a terror. I started to train him about a week after getting him, once he had settled in. I started with the 'stay' and 'come' commands. I would put him on a spot and ask him to stay, but of course he would wander because he had no idea at first what I wanted from him. When I asked him to stay he would go and pee in the corner, sniff the rubbish bin, crawl under the sofa or roll over for me to tickle his belly.

The first few days, there didn't seem to be any progress; but I knew if I persevered, change would come – and it did. After a few more days of just two 10-minute sessions a day, he started to understand what I wanted from him. Initially he would stay for a few seconds, but gradually he would stay until I commanded him to come. He was getting it.

The reason I was training him was not just to make my life easier, but a trained dog, in my view, is a happy dog – and it is the same with our minds. A mind that is trained, or we could say a mind that is *present*, is a happy mind.

Thoughts of the Untrained Mind

A lot of the activities that distract an untrained puppy are fairly innocuous, such as tipping over a bin or peeing in the corner. But if not watched, they can be life-threatening – for example, the puppy could get out of the house and wander into the road, or start eating things it shouldn't. It is similar with our untrained minds. A lot of the time they may wander into areas that don't cause us too much distress, such as thinking about yesterday's dinner, or the holiday we would like to go on. But if we are not vigilant, our minds can take us to hell and back in less than a second. We may start thinking things like 'Nobody likes me,' or 'I will never amount to anything, my life is hopeless'. These are

*Patience gives us
perspective to carry on*

the kind of thoughts that can create enormous distress in our lives, and it is all self-inflicted. What I mean here is that the distress is created not by what is really happening, but by the belief that the thoughts in our heads are true.

If we go back to training the puppy, there are three qualities I had to employ while training him. The first one was compassion. If the puppy had disobeyed my commands and I had yelled at him, I would have ended up with a very frightened and unhealthy puppy. I had to treat him with compassion at all times. I didn't always want to – especially when he peed in the corner – but to show him that I was getting angry would have achieved nothing. The second quality was patience. I had to keep going, even though at times he didn't seem to be getting it. I knew deep down that eventually it would all click with him, if I remained compassionate and patient with his training. Patience gives us perspective to carry on. It allows us to see beyond the current situation to a time when things will be different. The third quality, which may surprise some people, was that of firmness. Even though I was compassionate and patient, I had to be firm with him. I had to let him know that I was not going to give up just because he wanted to play. There were times for playing later, of course, but training had to be done.

It is these three qualities that we need to bring to our mindfulness practice if we are going to succeed in training our minds – compassion, patience and firmness.

Patience

Let's look first at patience. We need patience because our minds will wander – just as it is in the nature of a puppy to wander, so it is the nature of our minds to think. We will never have a completely blank mind and that is not the point of mindfulness. We need patience because without it we will give ourselves a very hard time; our minds will continue to wander and think about all sorts of irrelevant things. It is true that our mind can become quieter and calmer over months and years of practising mindfulness, but it will never become completely still for very long. The reason patience is important is that it allows us to develop a healthy perspective on this very issue. Most of us start our mindfulness practice wanting to change our minds instantly so that we never think a bad thought again. But instead of trying to stop the mind from thinking, we begin to gain a little wisdom about the whole affair, which means we stop fighting a battle we will never win. Let me repeat that in a different way. If you come to mindfulness meditation with a wilful attitude to change yourself quickly, you will suffer as a consequence; you are creating a battle where there doesn't need to be one and you will only lose. Trying to change your mind wilfully is like trying to change the weather – impossible!

Trying to change your mind wilfully is like trying to change the weather – impossible!

Patience allows us to form a new relationship with what it is to be a human being. With patience, we begin to see that the best we can do is to accept completely that the mind, just like the weather, is beyond our control. The mind will wander; we can't stop this. So instead of trying to change our mind, we need to change our attitude toward it.

Compassion

This brings us to the quality of compassion. Compassion is not only a feeling of warmth or acceptance, it is an understanding that this moment is as it is. Compassion allows us to accept that we are as we are and that trying to be any different is not only painful but a great dishonour to ourselves. Compassion is the reassuring little smile to yourself when you are feeling confused and bewildered with life. Most of all, compassion is a welcoming space for everything about yourself that you may not like. It warms the often cold and critical attitude that we can have toward ourselves. Along with curiosity, it is the quality that melts the ice so we can have access to the jewel.

When we focus on the breath, for example, compassion is already realizing that the mind is going to wander and that this is actually fine with us. Compassion is bringing our focus gently back again, with an attitude that you would bring to the puppy in its training. To do otherwise is not only foolish but creates distress.

Firmness

Firmness or perseverance means not giving up. Mindfulness is not easy to begin with, so we need to be determined. We need to foster an energy that will give us a good start. It is similar to rowing a boat – we need to give ourselves a good push from the shore and keep going until we are taken by the current. Once we are in the current, it all becomes much easier. But until we are, we need to persevere.

Mindfulness is simple but difficult. It is the most uncomplicated activity we can engage in but also one of the most demanding to begin with. If we are going to succeed in our mindfulness journey, we will need plenty of patience, compassion and perseverance.

CHOICELESS AWARENESS

◆

Choiceless awareness is the way of mindfulness and effortlessness. It is a way of being at ease with ourselves rather than frantically trying to manipulate and control our experience into what we want it to be, or how we think it should be.

I SPENT MANY YEARS TRYING TO GET SOMEWHERE in meditation. I tried to be calm, I tried to feel good, I tried to have only positive thoughts. I tried very hard to get rid of all my 'bad' feelings and to have only 'good' ones, and I tried to get into higher states of consciousness. God loves a trier, they say, but it didn't seem to be doing me much good. Then I came across a teaching called Choiceless Awareness and I was intrigued – mainly because I was trying very hard to 'choose' my experience and it didn't seem to be bringing me much calm and joy. Choiceless awareness is a way of opening to experience rather than trying to control it. When we 'practise' choiceless awareness meditation, everything about ourselves is allowed to arise and to pass away in its own time and in its own way.

I realized that by bringing 'choicelessness' into my mindfulness practice, I was aligning myself with the natural way of things. The natural way is for all things to arise and to pass away. What I had been doing for many years in meditation was to deny the natural flow that is life. I realized I was frightened of life. Life isn't something we can hold on to, and if we try to do this it creates stress and suffering, because we are denying a simple but profound fact of life – what arises, passes. This is a core teaching of most religions. We could say that meditation is waking up to the facts of life – that which comes into being will eventually pass away. But we don't want to hear this; we ignore this. We want to think that we are a fixed and separate being and not part of life, but a-part from life, even though we long to be at one with it. Our efforts go into maintaining this sense of a fixed and permanent entity and it uses up a lot of our energy, often leaving us exhausted. We're fighting a losing battle.

We not only want ourselves to be fixed and unchanging (even though paradoxically we want to change), we want all that brings us pleasure and comfort in life, such as possessions and reputation, to remain the same. However, when we hold on to things emotionally, the result is pain because the law of nature is that what appears also disappears. When we grasp after pleasure, the possibility of pain is always there. If we attach to pleasure, we will get pain too; but if we can welcome pleasure and indeed enjoy it without grasping, then pain does not arise. This is something we all have to work out for ourselves in our own experience.

Let It Be

I remember how for years I had the view that to be happy and peaceful I had to keep any unhappy thoughts and any unpeaceful feelings out of my experience. What I was actually doing was repressing energy and aspects of myself that wanted to follow the flow of life, to arise into consciousness and pass away. Fortunately, I came across teachers who had been through the same process and were wise and compassionate enough to pass on what they had learned.

I realized that peacefulness isn't something that I can create through choosing what to experience. I had to have the courage to open to all of my experience and to let it be. Letting it be means allowing it into awareness. It means to feel what I may not want to feel because I have a view that it's bad, for whatever reason. Letting things be isn't passive. It means being gently curious about what is happening in the body, feeling all the tensions, all the tight areas; it means feeling all the open and expansive parts, too. We bring things into awareness and that's all that we need to do. We cannot trust that life will always be what we want it to be, but we can trust in awareness of it.

Spacious Awareness

We cannot simply open ourselves in a flash – it takes patience, compassion and sensitivity toward ourselves. But if we are willing to be choiceless, more and more, as time goes on, we will see a change. We realize that the peace we were striving for by trying to control our experience happens when we don't need to control our experience any more.

Many of us intuitively know that there is something about us that is boundless, limitless and joyful. In our opening image, we can see this as the jewel. However, when we turn back to our experience, we certainly don't see ourselves as boundless, limitless and joyful. Often our experience is just the opposite. We can experience ourselves as very limited and unhappy. However, the limitless and joyful has not gone away, but has simply been covered over by views, desires and fears that we spend half our time following and the other half battling against. The unbounded and joyful is our true nature and is not a thing in itself. It is like the sky. The sky exists but is not

a thing in itself – it is the absence of things, but yet it exists. You cannot grab the sky and put it in your pocket, nor can you bottle it, but it's there.

Anything & Everything

The intuitive sense of boundlessness and at the same time the experience of pain and limitation is often referred to as the holy war – this being a war between stagnation and growth. The more we open and listen intuitively to the call of the unlimited, the more it manifests in our life. But we must also work with the limited. We must face the fears, desires and anxieties that we have as humans on this earth. This is where being choiceless is helpful. When we practise choiceless awareness, we let go of any object or focus of meditation. We observe anything and everything as it arises. We observe any judgements and opinions and let them pass by like clouds in the sky. We watch and listen to any uncertainty and doubts about how we are doing. We notice thoughts and bodily sensations as they arise into awareness and watch those change, too. In other words, we are choiceless about what we give our attention to.

We don't give something attention on the grounds that we want more of it because it is pleasant, or less of it because it is unpleasant. We give our attention to something because it is there. Because by being with that something, we learn to be at ease with it rather than reacting to it.

EXERCISE

CHOICELESS AWARENESS

Below is a meditation to help you practise choiceless awareness. This is a practice you can do for 10–15 minutes once or twice a week if it appeals to you. The emphasis, rather than being on the breath or body, is on whatever comes into your space of awareness without having an agenda to change it, get rid of it, judge it or anything else. Of course, if we do any of these, that is just noticed too. You cannot do this wrong – you just need a willingness. Your attitude is simply to notice what comes into your space of awareness.

- Take up your meditation posture.

- In awareness now there is a sense of the body – with all its sensations. You may notice the breath coming and going. Just observe and experience what comes into your awareness.

- Maybe there are thoughts about whether you are doing it correctly or not – just notice. Give up control.

- Perhaps there are feelings of agitation or feelings of calm … Allow everything to be in your space of awareness … Welcome it all compassionately.

- Perhaps you notice being lost in thoughts – absolutely fine … Just relax – because there is no special way to do this … Everything is noticed …

- You may have doubts – good, just observe them … Everything has its place. If you find yourself wanting a better experience, that is welcome too.

- Just let each moment unfold as it is … Relax … because there is nothing to DO …

- When the time is up, take a few moments and then, when you are ready, get on with your day.

However, if the urge to get rid of something unpleasant arises, that, too, is given space and allowed to follow its course. The practice of choiceless awareness is the opening to nature's way – that life appears in certain forms for a while, changes and passes away. As this becomes clearer to us, we see that there is no permanency to any of our experience, and that none of this really belongs to us – it just happens. Just like the heart beats, the blood flows and the body breathes without any effort on our part. This is a liberating experience and brings a great sense of ease.

Noticing Space

Mindfulness allows us to sit at ease with the flow of emotions, thoughts and images that pass through our being. We see more clearly nature's law – that all is changing moment by moment. But we also see something else that we had ignored all our lives – we begin to notice space.

When I walk into a room, I immediately notice the objects in the room. I notice curtains, carpets, chairs and maybe people. I notice the walls with pictures hanging and I notice the ceiling. What I don't notice is the space. It is the same with my mind. I notice the 'objects' – thoughts, images and memories. However, through practising mindfulness, we gradually gain a sense of the natural spaciousness of our own mind, which is the purpose of choiceless meditation. This brings with it a sense of ease, because we begin to realize that there is 'something' other than thoughts that we can rely on. It may not be something tangible, like a chair or a house, but it is definitely there. This is an intuitive awareness of space. We can sit and think about this spaciousness for decades and we will still be no nearer to understanding it. However, once we begin to trust this spaciousness – which is our natural intelligence – we then start to loosen our attachment to thoughts, and this is one of the greatest blessings we can experience.

STABILITY, STILLNESS & DEPTH

We all want stability in our lives, but for many of us it seems an elusive quality. We may appear stable to the outside world but our internal life is in turmoil. Our thoughts give rise to emotions that leave us confused, uncertain what to do or how to act.

WE MAY ATTEMPT TO GAIN SOME STABILITY by trying to be a good person or having a wonderful personality and 'doing the right thing' so that everybody likes us. We do this so we won't have to feel any pain. This, however, only leads to frustration and leaves us even further from stability.

We may attempt to find some stability by immersing ourselves in pleasant experiences and trying to keep anything unpleasant out of our lives. This way only leads to tension and leaves us nervously looking out for anything that may threaten our pleasant life.

Looking for stability using this approach is like trying to find calm on the surface of the ocean. It is not going to happen, at least not for long.

To find stability on an ocean, a ship has a keel, which reaches down beneath the choppy surface to the depths of the ocean. Without the keel, the ship would be tossed around on the surface like a little boat; but instead of being tossed around or fighting against the waves, the ship rides the waves – it moves with them.

The Keel in Our Lives

What is the keel in our lives? The keel, that which brings stability, is awareness. It is the willingness to open to and allow our experience to reveal itself. Often when something unpleasant goes on in our lives, we 'run away' and find comfort in over-drinking, overworking or other behaviours to avoid discomfort. It is good to know our strategies. Keeping unpleasantness away may seem a sensible thing to do and to an extent, of course, it is – we don't go looking for it; but the nature of life is that some unpleasantness or pain will come our way. It is a fact of life – so we need to grow up and learn to face it head on.

When unpleasant emotions arise within us, the keel is our ability to experience the emotion in the body. Often when we are feeling discomfort, we disappear into our head and try to work it out, or we blame somebody for making us feel that way, or even blame ourselves. This fans the flames of the emotions. Stability does not mean that we don't have emotions and feelings but that we can learn to experience them in the body, here and now. In a way, we learn to be with them, to be compassionate towards them, and not be tossed about by them.

When feeling something unpleasant, such as anxiety, fear or sadness, our work is to move toward it and feel it. Be curious about it, be kind, notice where you feel it, notice its different qualities. If we can do this without getting lost in thinking, the emotion tends to dissipate. It is like the calm at the end of a storm.

Finding Stability

Awareness is also the stillness. We bring the agitated emotion into the stillness of awareness and allow it to burn itself out. Awareness here can be likened to a large paddock where wild horses are tamed. The paddock contains the horse until the horse tires and calms down. The emotion 'tires' because we are not feeding it with lots of unconscious thinking about what caused it or how to get rid of it. All that thinking is the mind's way of taking us away from feeling anything unpleasant.

After having done this several times, we may come to see that even in the midst of strong emotions we can still have a sense of stability and of stillness. Stillness is not the absence of agitation and upset, but rather how we relate to it.

We develop and strengthen stability, stillness and depth through meditation by commitment and consistent practice. It's not really about effort but more about a *willingness* to welcome whatever arises to our awareness. I may be sitting in meditation or in my daily life and feel fear or anxiety. I can try to oppose this or I can ask the question, 'What's this?' or 'What does this feel like?' I am then more likely to turn toward and give space to this uncomfortable emotion. If I do that for a while, I notice that the emotion of fear no longer upsets me like it used to.

We strengthen stability, stillness and depth through meditation by commitment and consistent practice

I become more stable in the face of strong emotion. Through facing my uncomfortable emotions this way, I find that I identify less with the waves of emotion and more with my capacity to experience them. This brings a deeper stillness to my being than I experienced previously.

It is similar with depth. Whereas before I would identify and get upset because of the emotional turbulence, I now have confidence in my ability to experience it because I am in touch with something far deeper than the emotion itself. It is almost like I now have roots that are not very easily shaken. This is because I have become willing to turn toward my experience instead of running away and distracting myself whenever the slightest insecure tremble rocks my boat.

The Changing-ness of Life

However, there is another element in all this that we need to give attention to. We develop stability, stillness and depth by seeing life as it really is, rather than how we think it should be. In other words, we need to be open to the facts of life – and as we have seen, one of the facts of life, and maybe the most important, is that everything changes. That everything changes is something we can rely on; it is a truth in which we can absolutely trust. In other words, we can rely on the *awareness* that everything changes. Our only certainty, then, is the 'changing-ness' of life. This can sound quite depressing, but, actually, what is depressing is that we battle and resist the way life is. We try to hold on to loved ones, we try to hold on to our status and reputation, our good name. We try to hold on to anything that gives us excitement or pleasure. I know myself when I listen to some good music and there is a great crescendo toward the end, I don't want it to stop, I want it to keep going. I do not want to let go and be in the gap left by that sound.

Opening to the fact that everything changes allows stability and stillness into our lives. We become stable because we are not relying on our own false views that life will remain the same. We have become comfortable with the fact that every-thing changes; this also brings stillness to our minds, because we no longer fear the changing-ness of life. This is true stabil-ity, stillness and depth.

How Do I Know
Meditation is Working?

◆

The criterion many people use to assess if their meditation is working is if it feels 'good'. If it feels uncomfortable in some way, they judge it as 'bad' because it isn't pleasant. However, whether the meditation was pleasant or not is really irrelevant.

I AM OFTEN ASKED: 'How do I know my meditation is work-ing?' What people often do to see if their meditation is working is to look at it, which seems logical. If your car isn't working, you look at your car. If your phone stops working, you look at your phone. This approach seems sensible enough, and it is with most things – but not with meditation.

When asked this question, I ask people to look at their everyday lives to see if the meditation is working, and more specifically at their relationships. If, over time, our relation-ships are not changing – if we are not becoming a little kinder, a little more empathic, a little less anxious – then our medita-tion is not working. Meditation is not about having a nice, relaxing time on the cushion, it's about changing your life.

Opening the Second Door

Imagine a room with two doors. Door A is always open, door B is usually closed. Imagine also a queue of people at door A, entering into the room. The people never stop entering, the queue is moving constantly – so, as you can see, at some point the room starts to get overcrowded. It becomes very claustrophobic and sooner or later even the walls come under strain. I wonder what happens next in your scenario?

As you may have guessed, the room represents ourselves. The open door A represents life and life never stops happening; that is why the people never cease entering the room. The closed door B represents our unwillingness to experience life as it is. I am talking here mainly of the more painful emotions, such as fear, anger, sadness, grief, etc. We close door B because we feel that life is too much or that there is something wrong with feeling like this.

Mindfulness and compassion practice is not about trying to close the first door so that we don't feel anything unpleasant – it is about opening the second door. All emotions want simply to be experienced for a duration then allowed to pass away. This is healthy and brings an ease of being and a joy to life. However, we tend to make a problem out of emotions that seem threatening. We don't like to feel sad, for example,

All emotions want simply to be experienced for a duration then allowed to pass away

because we may appear weak, or it seems to point to something being wrong and life not going our way. So what we do when difficult emotions show their little heads is to attempt to shove them back down again; we close the door on them.

Busyness is the height

of laziness; it stops us from

seeing what is really going on.

TRADITIONAL BUDDHIST SAYING

But if we keep closing the door on our emotions, at some point the 'walls' will come under strain and – well, we know what may happen next.

Seasoning the Soul

We open the second door by compassionately turning toward the emotions that arise in the body; by giving them space and keeping the door open, we then allow them to pass on. Sadness, for example, is a natural response to some events in life and actually 'seasons our soul' – in other words, it can mature us as human beings. Sadness opens our hearts to allow others to enter. This opening of our hearts to others is the blossoming of compassion. Experiencing sadness connects us to others because the wisdom of experience shows us that we all suffer sadness. Sadness and pain are not some sort of mistake, they are essential – if there were no pain and sorrow, there would be no connection and compassion. They reveal our common humanity. If we close the door on sadness, we remain locked away in our own little experience of life and the result is emotional claustrophobia.

When we shut out sadness and other experiences, we also shut out something else, and that something else is joy and happiness. Most people think that if they keep hurtful or sad feelings out of awareness that they will be well, but this is not the case. To experience the joy of life, we need to be able to experience the sadness of life too.

Our work with mindfulness is firstly to observe how we turn away from painful emotions and allow thoughts to run rampant in our minds. We can then take our attention away from the thoughts and into the felt experience of the emotions in the body. To open the door means to experience life moment by moment, whether it be joy or sorrow – because they are the same. They are like two sides of the same coin: if you throw one side of a coin away, the other goes with it.

CHAPTER TWO

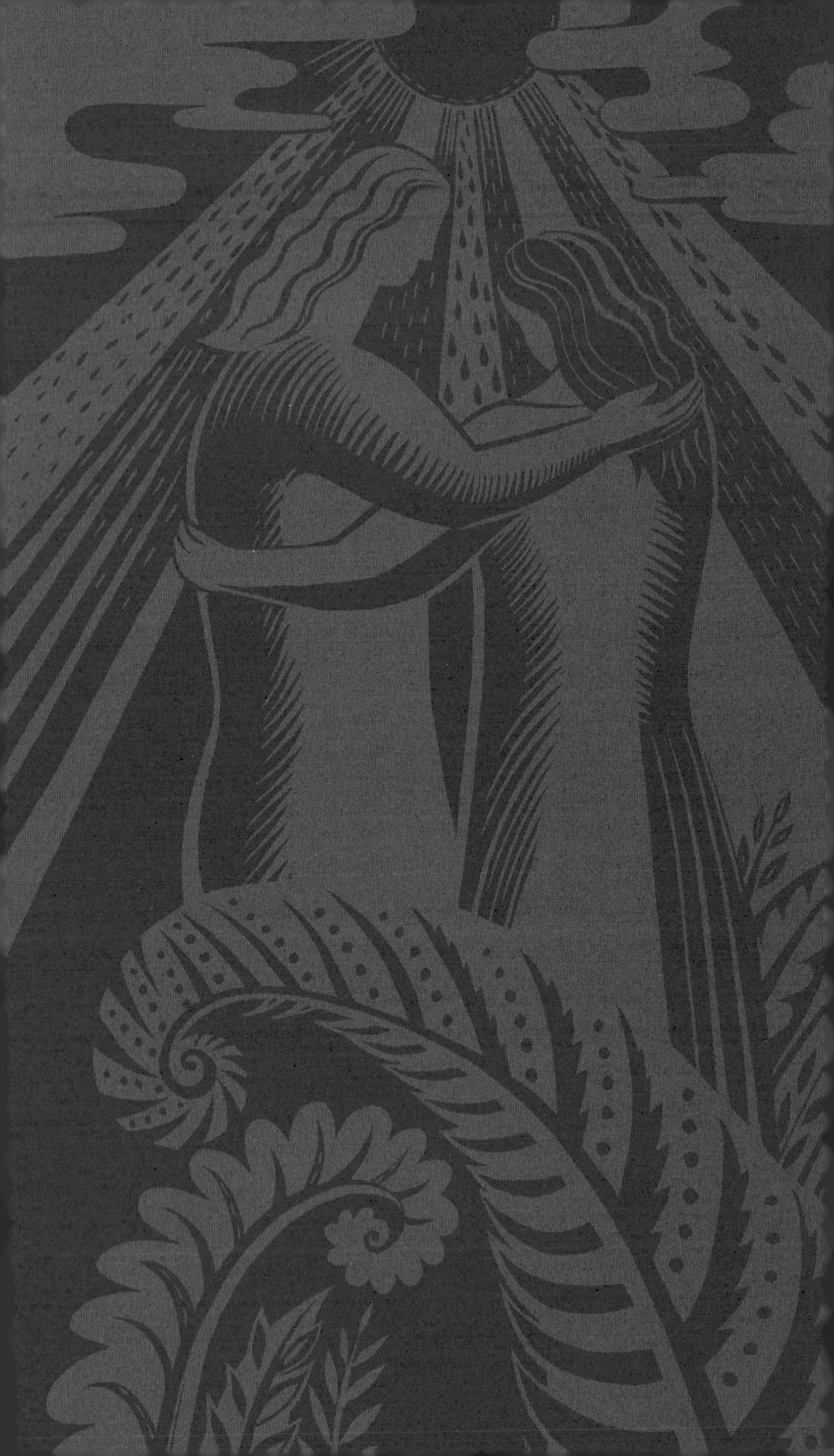

ENDING THE TYRANNY OF THOUGHTS

According to the latest research, people spend 46.9 per cent of their waking time thinking about something other than what they are doing.[2] The research goes on to say that this wandering mind is making people unhappy. A lot of the thinking, or mind chatter, dwells on things that have happened in the past or that may or may not happen in the future. This mind chatter is a kind of tyranny which can keep us agitated, anxious and ill at ease.

THE CRITICAL VOICE

◆

Many of us have a critical voice inside telling us we are stupid, selfish, weird, ugly, lonely, or unlovable. It sits in our head all day long, giving out its opinions about everything we do. It can make our lives a misery — so how do we silence it?

I REMEMBER TIMES IN MY LIFE when the critic was almost unbearable. I didn't dare speak at dinner parties because I believed that nobody would find me interesting. The critic would use slightly different methods at different times to get me to behave. Initially, it would just be a subtle feeling of *I shouldn't do this* or *They will just laugh at me.* One of my critic's favourite lines was: *They will just laugh at you, don't show yourself up.* Other times, if I dared to disobey, it would start shouting at me or even screaming: *You idiot, they are not interested in you, sit down and shut up. What the hell have you got to say that is interesting?*

The critic left me feeling cut off from the world around me. It would criticize me for not being generous enough, then when I did something generous, it would criticize me because I was making a fool of myself and people would just take advantage. It would even enter into my meditation practice. *You are not trying hard enough, everybody else on retreat is getting somewhere.* It would fill my head full of thoughts then criticize me for having a headful of thoughts. The consequences of having a strong inner critic were that I felt unlovable and rather useless at almost everything – except sport. For whatever reason, it didn't seem to enter into my sporting life. I played tennis, squash and badminton and was rather good at them. The critic didn't seem concerned with that area of my life. It was more concerned with my relationships to other people and how they viewed me.

The Spectre of the Inner Critic

It's very easy to be both very successful in life and completely miserable. They often go together – not always, of course, but often. The reason for this is the spectre of the inner critic – because no matter how successful we become, the critic will not stop. Its *job* is to criticize and, like all of us, it doesn't want to be out of a job. Even the most successful person can become depressed under its relentless attack.

The inner critic is an impostor, but ignoring it and the emotions it generates doesn't generally work. Nor does criticizing yourself for ignoring your feelings, as we know whose voice that is. The critic can paralyze you, then criticize you for feeling paralyzed. It is expert at finding your tender spots.

Your inner critic sometimes means well, but often it does not. In my one-to-one work with people, I have met some critics whose purpose is to make the person utterly miserable. I say the critic is an impostor because it normally rears its head in childhood or in teenage years. We are not born with a raging critic; but we can struggle for years against it and get nowhere.

So how do we free ourselves from the critical voice? The dilemma of how to work with the critic has been a long-term endeavour for me. I think a lot of us would rather it just disappeared off the face of the earth. Many of us try ignoring it and the emotions it generates, or maybe even arguing with it. I haven't found these methods very useful, however. In fact, I haven't come across a sure way of dealing with the inner critic that suits everybody. For some, meditation is sufficient and that is the way I mainly worked through it. Other people I know have explored what the critic wants and have managed to placate it. Others still have attended workshops where they have drawn the critic, created a clay image of it, and dialogued with it, which has helped them.

The Beautiful Art of Unhooking

One way to approach the issue is to learn the beautiful art of unhooking yourself from your thoughts. Imagine you are fishing. You bait a hook, then throw it into the water, where it waits for the fish to bite. Along comes the fish, which gobbles up the bait, then bites into the hook. What happens next is interesting – the more the fish struggles, the deeper the hook goes. The fish wriggles and flaps, but the hook goes deeper still.

Thoughts are like hooks. They come along, we 'bite' on them and they hook us. The more we struggle against them, the deeper the hook goes. We often struggle with thoughts such as 'I hate thinking like this', or we argue with the critic and try to convince ourselves the voice is not true. All these thoughts are just more hooks and our wriggling to break free only entangles us more. The pull of the hook – of the thoughts, of the inner critic – only gets stronger.

The real reason the critic stays around is that we choose to believe what it says. If we stopped believing it, the critic would lose its power.

The art of unhooking yourself means you stop fighting the thoughts, you stop arguing with the inner critic because this doesn't work. You stop the fight and there's space to free yourself, to unhook yourself from these thoughts. You do so by letting your thoughts drift away and coming back to the here and now. Come back to what is really happening. All those stories in our heads just create distress. Learn the art of letting go and coming back to whatever you are doing. If you are meditating, then come back to the breath; if you are chopping a carrot, come back to that; if you are listening to a friend, come back to that. We come back to the activity we are engaged in because it is real – but the stories in our heads take us to somewhere that doesn't really exist.

Functional Thoughts

The thoughts I am talking about are the ones that stampede through our heads with views, opinions and judgements. However, we don't need to treat all thoughts like this, as some are useful. The useful thoughts we can, of course, listen to,

then decide to act on them, or not. These I call functional thoughts, and the way to identify them is that they do not create emotional upset. The more confident you are in your mindfulness practice, the easier it becomes to tell the difference between the thoughts of a critic, for example, and thoughts that are useful. What I suggest here is to notice the *tone* of thought. The critic's voice has an edge to it, and is normally absolute – it thinks it knows and tends to repeat itself. Ask yourself: 'Does this voice feel kind?' If it is the critic, you will tend to notice a corresponding feeling or contraction in the body. Basically, we can see that this whole show is going on in our head. This is what I call 'false emotion' – the emotion the critic creates is false because whatever it is saying is not actually happening. Thoughts that are useful or functional will not have the same emotional charge.

Counting Your Thoughts

Counting our thoughts tends to stop them, giving us a second or two of head space. Try it now – just count your thoughts as they come along. When we count our thoughts, we have a perspective on them rather than being caught up in them. In a sense, we step off the wheel of unconscious thinking – we become conscious of our thoughts. Don't be surprised here if you do have a blank mind for a few seconds.

THE SILENT MIND

✦

We could say that to have a silent mind is what meditation is really about. It is the source of joy, wisdom, compassion and creativity, and the end of sorrow as we know it. But what is a silent mind, and how do we achieve one?

A SILENT MIND IS NOT A BLANK MIND where nothing ever happens. It is not a mind where we do not have any thoughts and feelings. It is not fuzzy; it's not a dull mind where we cannot think straight. A silent mind is alive; it is clear and unclouded by fear and craving. Thoughts arise, but there is little attachment to them and they are not taken personally. For example, we may have thoughts such as 'My life is hopeless' or 'I am a bad person'. Normally when these thoughts appear in our minds, we are

A silent mind is alive; it is clear and unclouded by fear and craving

utterly convinced that they speak the truth about us, and so they generate feelings of us being bad, doing wrong or being unlovable. We may then believe that the way forward is to just try and think the opposite. This, however, is just to get caught up in the whole 'positive thinking' approach and does not really work. Trying to build a healthy, solid sense of self out of thought is always doomed to failure because thoughts have a life all of

All of humanity's problems

stem from man's inability to

sit quietly in a room alone.

BLAISE PASCAL (1623–62)
FRENCH PHILOSOPHER

their own. Negative thoughts will always appear out of nowhere, demolishing our thought-made world.

Thoughts of this nature have absolutely no purpose but to make us feel miserable and separate from others. In the silent mind they are allowed to arise and to pass away without causing a ripple. The silent mind is a happy mind. It is happy because it is unaffected by the debris of thoughts that pass through it. The silence doesn't judge, doesn't criticize. That which judges is the judgemental mind, that which criticizes is the critical mind. The silent mind remains unaffected by whatever enters into it. It responds to life not from fear, hatred and craving but from wisdom and compassion. Most of our thinking is unconscious, and if we believe the thoughts that pass through our minds we will suffer, because most of our unconscious thinking is negative in nature. The attachment to and the belief in thought is very strong because it's the source of our identity. We would much rather be a somebody who suffers than a nobody who is happy, because a somebody who suffers attracts more attention.

The silent mind is not our personal creation, it is our natural state. It doesn't belong to us as a personal possession. This is good news, because if we possessed it then we could lose it. But we cannot lose what we don't possess.

Trust in the Stillness…

The silent mind is a simple mind. Often our clever and busy minds complicate our lives. Thinking is a great tool that we can employ when necessary, but it has taken control and believes it can sort out our lives for us, when actually it is part of the problem. The silent mind doesn't confuse us, it brings serenity and love. It is something we can trust in absolutely. We cannot trust in our drama-ridden personalities, but we can trust in the stillness that contains it all.

Through mindfulness meditation, we can learn to recognize this stillness. We can come to see the difference between thinking and the awareness of thinking. If we persevere, we will come to experience the still, alive presence 'behind' the thinking mind. The silent mind simply watches, it doesn't get involved in the whole drama of the personality. It's not that there is anything wrong with the personality, it's just that if we rely on it then we tend to get confused, because different aspects of the personality believe and want different things. We can go through life believing that we *are* the personality, when actually we are the peaceful, compassionate presence that embraces the personality. The personality is conditioned.

My personality – which is sometimes a bit weird, I must say – is different from your personality because our conditioning is different. Someone from a different culture will have a different kind of personality, with different likes and dislikes. There is nothing wrong with this and there is no judgement about it. It becomes a problem when we start thinking that there is something wrong with it, or that there is something wrong with somebody else because they believe and do things differently to us. If we are in touch with our true nature then we accept our personality, with all its quirks and foibles.

…And Trust in Awareness

Our work in meditation and in daily life is to loosen our attachments to our thoughts. To trust in the very simple act of awareness. Throughout the day, we can come to see how believing in thoughts can actually drive us mad. We are not judging thoughts here, but simply paying attention to them. We may have thoughts like 'I'm no good' but we can learn to let these thoughts go and not take them seriously. If we have thoughts that seem to have some significance, then through paying attention we can respond to them. For example, I may have a thought like, 'I was pretty horrible to so-and-so last night, I could apologize.' If that feels right, then I can choose to do something about it. Through awareness of thoughts, we intuitively learn to listen to the wise ones and ignore the ones that cause distress.

If we are controlled by the judgemental and the critical mind, they can make our lives hellish. We will find that we have opinions and judgements about all kinds of things that simply don't matter. The critical mind can criticize us for feeling sad and for feeling happy. It can criticize us for feeling greedy and feeling generous. The critical mind doesn't allow us to feel at ease because it's always being critical of whatever our experience is. We can so easily get into feeling: 'I shouldn't feel sad, what will people think of me?' So we put on a brave face and feel insincere instead.

The critical mind can criticize us for feeling sad and for feeling happy

The silent mind allows everything to be what it is. It allows sadness to arise and pass away without judgement, it allows all moods to be as they are without making a problem out of them. We don't need to try to cultivate the silent mind, but we do need to let go of all the noise – the opinions, judgements, criticisms and resistances to what is happening right here and now. Our struggles have little to do with the contents of our minds, but rather with our judgements about those contents. As we let thoughts be and rest in awareness rather than blindly following them, we can begin to sense an alive stillness behind all the activity.

When we are more aware of the silent mind, our struggles gradually begin to diminish and over time we will experience more ease and aliveness.

MINDFULNESS AND COMPASSION

Don't Take Your
Thoughts Personally

❖

A meditation teacher once told me that one of the most effective ways
of dealing with thoughts is to stop believing them, to learn not to
take them so seriously. Recognizing our thoughts for what they are
— a mental event — is an act of compassion to oneself.

IT IS SO EASY TO BELIEVE our thoughts on any situation in our
lives. We believe they are the angels of wisdom and we can
trust them. But this is not the case. Thoughts can tell us that we
are no good – this is both true and untrue. Thoughts can tell us
we cannot do something – this is both true and untrue. They tell
us we are unlovable – this too is true and untrue. They can tell
us that we will be alone for ever, that we may never find a good
job, that we are better or worse than other people – these are
both true and untrue. What I mean is that if we believe them, they
will *appear* to be true for us. For example, if we have the thought
that we are unlovable, then we will experience that to be true and
feel and act that way. But if that thought is seen and not believed,
it has no power. We are then free from its tyranny.

This is why labelling thoughts in mindfulness practice is
essential. When we have thoughts that are charged with emotion, we can label them as anxious thoughts, angry thoughts,
fantasy thoughts, panic thoughts, fearful thoughts or blaming
thoughts. In this way, we get to know our own mind and see

Labelling Thoughts

Take your attention to your breath and follow its rhythm. Notice when you get distracted by thoughts, and instead of criticizing yourself for getting lost in thinking, just say to yourself, 'Thinking'. When you have drifted off, there is always a moment when you 'pop' back to the here and now. At that moment, just say again to yourself, 'Thinking', and return your attention to the body and the breath. We will often start criticizing ourselves for 'drifting off', but by simply observing the thinking itself and not reacting in any way, we begin to relax, and joy enters our lives.

just how repetitive it is. As we do this, another thing gradually takes place – these thoughts lose their power over us. In other words, the ice surrounding the jewel begins to melt. This is because once we notice and label them, we give them no more attention and in fact take our attention back to the body and breath or whatever it is we are doing at that moment.

The Mindful Life

If we live in the world of these stampeding thoughts, we are forever restless and unhappy. We can liken our minds to the ocean. There are the waves on the surface, always moving, never really still; this is the level of thought. But there are also the depths of

the ocean, with all its power and beauty. The depths are still and rich with life. It is the same with us. Once we live free from the dictates of our thoughts, we tap into something that is wiser and richer – more satisfying and fulfilling just in itself. We find ourselves happier and more content, for no reason.

This is the mindful life. It is a life where we notice our thoughts but learn not to take them too seriously. We learn to be aware of whatever sounds, smells, sights, tastes and sensations are present. When we pay attention in this way, we learn something very

The Mind Going for a Walk

When we have been sitting in a stuffy office for a long time, we like to get up and stretch, maybe go for a walk and get some fresh air. Well, it is the same with the mind. The mind, too, needs to go for a walk. It needs to be active. The reason it is so restless is that it is seeking something. It is trying to work out the best way to avoid any sort of pain. It is trying to protect you but making a pretty bad job of it.

Seeing the mind's need to go for a walk is a good way of approaching meditation. The mind doesn't like meditation because we are subtly asking it to calm down and be quiet, but rather than getting annoyed at it for thinking about this, that and the other thing, think of it as needing a walk. Give up the battle of trying to discipline it with effort; you will never win.

valuable – the difference between true emotion, which is created through contact with life as it is, and false emotion, which is created through believing our thoughts.

Letting Go of Baggage

Often in meditation, our aim is to feel good and to get rid of anything that feels bad, so our attention is on how we want to be rather than on how we are. But our attention needs to return from this idea of the future; it needs to be on what's happening here and now. This is all about making the unconscious conscious. What we are unconscious of, unaware of, is actually running our lives. For example, if we have been taught that anger is unacceptable, we can very easily get into repressing it (and make no mistake, we all experience anger) and it will leak out in other unconscious ways, like a seepage.

In meditation, we can allow ourselves to bring up our secret thoughts, views and opinions that we have been told are not acceptable. We can allow them space to arise into awareness, show them a little kindness, and this in itself is enough to let them go. We cannot let go of that of which we are not aware. We are not trying to get rid of it, or to change it into something else, but to allow it space to reveal itself. The same goes for anything else that is hidden away in the corners of our being. If we find we are afraid of something or somebody (and, by the way, it's OK to be afraid), we allow that to reveal itself. This is the way to be free of the baggage we all carry around. It is the way to happiness.

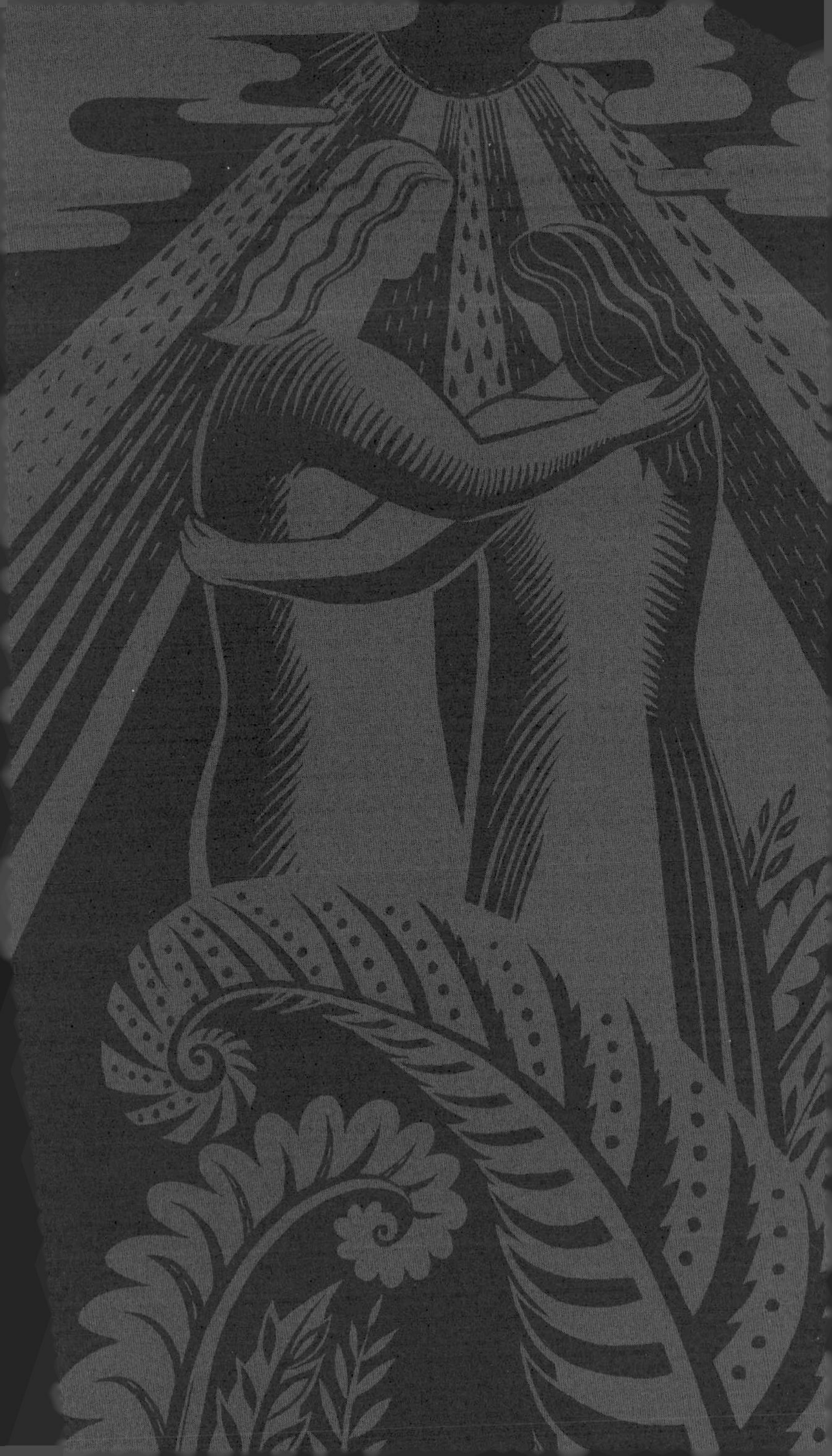

CHAPTER THREE

DANCING WITH DRAGONS

The dragon is one of the most common and enduring of mythical creatures. This fire-breathing demon represents in ourselves what we cannot face, what we are afraid of. Feelings and emotions don't begin life as dragons — we turn them into dragons through our fear of them, when what they really want is to be acknowledged and loved. This is what transforms negative emotions into allies, dragons into princes. We need to stop running away from the dragons and instead learn to dance with them. We need to learn the dragon dance.

UNACKNOWLEDGED SADNESS

Long after we have experienced deep loss of any kind and our grieving period has passed, the sadness can still remain. It remains in the shadows, often reminding us in moments of quiet that it is still there, just needing our acknowledgement.

WHEN I WAS A TEENAGER, crying came quite easily to me. It didn't take much to get the 'waterworks' going. A sad movie or an animal in distress touched me deeply. I was a sensitive young thing. I have a clear memory of walking around a local market with my mum and seeing this lovely old gentleman sitting behind his stall doing absolutely no business, while all the other stallholders seemed to be doing plenty. My heart went out to him and I was on the verge of tears, just seeing this and feeling sad for him. I had no idea what the situation really was for him, but I knew how I felt.

As time went on and I got older and probably not wiser, something changed – I am not saying it's good or bad, but something changed. I noticed I was not as sensitive as I was as a teenager. I didn't seem to 'feel for' people as much as I used to. Once I reached my early thirties, I think the taps were very much turned off. It took a lot to set me to tears then.

That was until I went on a solitary meditation retreat. It was my second solitary and I was alone for two weeks in a lovely remote hut in the Welsh countryside. I had no idea that things

were going to get interesting. I was meditating for around four to five hours a day. Apart from that, I was doing very little, reading and taking a few walks. After about the fourth day I started to feel unsettled and couldn't quite understand why. I started to feel sad but kept up my routine of sitting and walking. During an evening meditation, something inside shifted and the tears started to flow. It wasn't exactly painful but the tears were flowing. I didn't know why, but intuitively I knew I didn't need to do anything. I have often trusted my intuition in situations like that. I know that I have to just get out of my head and let it happen.

For the next few days the tears came and went, and so did the sadness. In between bouts of sadness I actually felt very light and happy. Then the sadness would flow again; but I was getting kind of used to it and just let it flow the best I could. I wasn't unsettled by it now in the way I was at the beginning. The sadness slowly eased over the next few days and I felt very light as a result.

◆

Some of you say, 'Joy is the greater
than sorrow,' and others say, 'Nay, sorrow
is the greater.' But I say unto you, they are inseparable.
Together they come, and when one sits, alone
with you at your board, remember that the
other is asleep upon your bed. [3]

FROM 'THE PROPHET' BY KAHLIL GIBRAN (1883–1931)
LEBANESE POET

◆

Releasing Blocked Emotions

During the last day or so, it dawned on me that the sadness that I felt was emotion that I had been carrying around for years. It was the hurt of childhood and the hurt of loved ones leaving me. It was the hurt of my dad spending many months in hospital with burned feet when I was about six years old. In a nutshell, it was what I called unacknowledged sadness. It was sadness that I had ignored because I didn't want to experience it for various reasons.

The fact that this happened then and in the way it did didn't really surprise me – though it did a little, too. After all, I knew enough about meditation to realize that to release blocked emotion was one of its benefits. What was surprising is that I didn't realize I had 'all that sadness in me'. It makes perfect sense now, of course, after years of practice, as I hope I am just a little bit wiser.

I often recommend a solitary retreat to people who may be ready. It is useful to have a teacher or guide with whom you can discuss your readiness; but if you simply feel drawn to this kind of retreat, then I suggest you just try it and see. A solitary retreat allows us to feel and express things that are difficult while living our often busy lives. Some people I will advise to start with a weekend, while to others I may say, 'Just jump into a week or more.' Yet others may be better talking to a friend or a good therapist.

Embracing the Sadness

In my teaching and the leading of retreats, I see unacknowledged sadness a lot. We have all had experiences that have been painful and left their mark, and if we don't allow ourselves the space to 'work through' and release these experiences, they remain lodged in the body, often for decades. That is why, when teaching meditation, I emphasize compassionate awareness of the sensations in the body. It's so easy to spend the sitting time lost in your head fantasizing, or trying to control your experience so that you avoid feeling any uncomfortable emotions.

When I talk about unacknowledged sadness, almost everybody nods their head in agreement. We all know that it exists. Most of us, understandably so, are quite wary of touching and experiencing it. But to be happy and free, we must do just that. It may not be mindfulness that does it for you, but if you sense that you have unacknowledged sadness then I encourage you to befriend it in the safest and most compassionate way possible. It will make a huge difference to your level of happiness. If we don't attend to it, it can in some cases lead to depression. The human body seems equipped to deal with a certain amount of held emotion but the threshold level varies between individuals.

How we approach this whole issue in meditation is crucial to whether we heal our lives or not. We can meditate for many years

and we may have been better off practising our swimming stroke. This is because we haven't actually engaged with ourselves and our pain. We have been too busy trying to get out of our experience by having a 'better' one.

The Element of Curiosity

When we meditate, one crucial element is often overlooked and that element is curiosity. When we meditate, we need to be curious. We take our place and we ask: 'What's happening?' This question, this curiosity helps us to remain present with our experience. This questioning rather than judging is an act of compassion to ourself. We may notice a tickle on the top lip, or a sensation of tingling in the hands. We may notice the sound of birds singing, or the patter of rain. If we remain curious, we come into the present moment and are alive to it. If you are willing to do this, you may even begin to sense some unacknowledged sadness. To experience this, little by little, is to heal your life and give happiness its rightful place.

In meditation, curiosity has two elements. One is the obvious definition of 'curious' – wanting to know what is happening. Through this element of curiosity, we discover sensations, sounds and thought patterns that we may previously only have been dimly aware of. The second element is being curious enough to stay with a sensation/feeling so as to allow it to unfold. This is where it gets very interesting, and it is often what many of us don't want to do, or don't value because we have an agenda

to change ourselves. Trying to change ourselves is an act of unkindness but being aware of ourselves is an act of compassion.

If we remain with a sensation (a tightness, a heaviness or whatever) and stay curious, we begin to sense new things about it. We may notice it tightening, or loosening and relaxing. We may notice an image associated with it. Perhaps we sense an emotion connected with it and feel flushed or a little nervous. How it unfolds is slightly different for each of us. But the healing happens if we stay there with gentleness and compassion. The key is – *wanting to know a little more about it*. Tears may begin to flow, or not.

Generational Pain

Most of the sadness we meet in our practice is personal, meaning that it arises out of the events of our own life. However, there is another level of sadness that is not really personal at all. It has nothing to do with how you have lived your life. This is what we could call generational sadness or generational pain, as it's not confined to sadness. This is the pain and sadness passed down through previous generations. This is pain that has not been resolved by our parents, grandparents, and even earlier ancestors. It may also be cultural or social pain that a society has not come to terms with. We may have had parents or ancestors who suffered from alcoholism, or were abused. We may have had grandparents who suffered during the terrible world wars. The list of 'reasons why' is endless, of course, and we don't need to know why.

What can be interesting is that, as children, we start out as 100 watt bulbs, full of love, warmth and enthusiasm. But if the family as a unit is shining at only 40 watts, then the child has to shrink in wattage to fit in – and the child must fit in. This shrinking down, however, can be the cause of great pain and sadness in later life, as some of us know from our own lives.

There are various therapies for dealing with generational pain. One of the best I have come across is *Family Constellations*, pioneered by Bert Hellinger. You can Google it and find a practitioner, if you are interested.

Sadness is not, of course, the only thing that meditation is concerned with. Its main purpose is to awaken us from spiritual ignorance. In other words, it is concerned with clarifying how we see ourselves and the world – because how we see the world is how we experience it.

SAD BUDDHA, HAPPY BUDDHA

◆

A Buddha is simply someone who is awake. He or she is not a god,
but a person who is awake to how things are, to how life is. We, too,
can be awake. When we are sad, we can be sad; when we are happy,
we can be happy.

IN 2001, WHEN I HAD BEEN LIVING IN VAJRALOKA, a meditation
retreat centre in North Wales, for a few months, I had a
realization that shocked me. I realized I was in constant tension,
and this was because I did not want to let life be as it was. I was
holding to my view of how things *should* be. I was clinging
desperately to how I thought I should be, and this was the cause
of distress in my life.

Knowing how I *should* be is easy. I should be more confident, more compassionate, wiser. I should be more open,
relaxed and always there for others. I should be calm, consistent and generous – oh, and I should be witty and liked by

◆

Life presents us with lessons all the time. It's better
if we learn each one, including the small ones. But we
don't want to learn them. We want to blame a problem
on somebody else, just brush it aside, or block it out.[4]

FROM 'NOTHING SPECIAL'
CHARLOTTE JOKO BECK WITH STEVE SMITH

◆

everybody. I realized that the list of how I should be was endless. I saw too that I always wanted to appear to be happy, which caused me much pain. I did my utmost never to appear sad or down, because this was not how I should be.

This, it seems to me, is in stark contrast to a Buddha. Someone who is awake doesn't resist life in any way; they are like a reed in the wind, and they bend with life rather than resist it. In this was a lesson for me and indeed a lesson for us all. If we look attentively and honestly at ourselves, we will see that we too are in constant tension. Always on red alert for anything that can hurt us. Physically, of course, this is completely natural and healthy. But the hurt we attempt to resist is more to do with how we appear to ourselves and the world. Our emotional life is the key. We are resistant to certain feelings and emotions because we are scared or because they don't fit in with the image we have of ourselves. This is why mindfulness in daily life is important, whether talking to a colleague, dressing the children or chopping an onion. Our daily life is our practice and embracing the emotions it throws up is our practice. This is what heals our lives from one of agitation and pain to one of contentment and joy. Instead of resisting sadness, anger and fear, we allow ourselves to feel them, to open compassionately to them.

Instead of resisting sadness, anger and fear, we allow ourselves to feel them

The Awakened Life

This is the awakened life – when you are sad, be a sad Buddha; when you are happy, be a happy Buddha. This goes for other emotions, too. When you are angry, be an angry Buddha; when you are calm, be a calm Buddha. This does not necessarily mean expressing anger, but rather noticing it, being mindful of it. In other words, what we can do is notice the thoughts that drive the emotion and bring awareness into the felt experience of anger in the body. Once we come out of thinking and in to the energy of anger in the body, it can begin to dissipate; but so long as we entertain thoughts like 'He shouldn't have said that, I'll get him back' or 'Nobody loves me', we will remain blinded by the anger or self-pity.

This is not repressing sadness or anger in any way. It is allowing it to be in our space of awareness, nothing more and nothing less. To be truly at peace, we need to stop running away from ourselves, we need to be honest about what is going on inside us. I am not asking you to *like* the feelings of anger or fear, but simply to let them be; those feelings are there, like them or not, so to deny them is to allow them to build up and explode at some later point. It is resisting the moment, and there is never peace where there is resistance.

Some years ago, I was leading a retreat when a woman spoke up and said, 'I'm just bored with all this sitting; nothing is happening.' I asked her to take away the label of boredom and to experience directly the energy in the body that she was

labelling. Later the same day she spoke again, saying, 'When I take away the label "boredom" I am not bored any more. I don't know what it is yet but it's not boredom; it's something else.' She had realized that she wasn't experiencing the moment but rather her thoughts about it. Having thoughts and opinions about the moment isn't experiencing it. Thoughts can be a part of momentary experience but often they are what we take to be reality. That is why I repeat again and again that, in meditation, our work is to be in this moment – whatever emotion or mood is present, just feel it. You may identify that you are sad or happy or anxious, but the most important thing is to experience it and stay with it. Notice how you want to think about something rather than experience life now. When we experience life *now*, there is no drama in it, no commentary about all that has gone wrong in the past and all that needs to go right in the future. When we truly experience the moment – not our opinions and judgements about it – there is happiness and peace.

To be aware and awake is not to be aware of something special. It is to be aware of your footsteps as you pass from one room to another. It is to be aware when tying your shoelaces or drinking your coffee. It is to be mindful of nodding in agreement with somebody when you don't really agree and it is being mindful of the compassionate or sad feelings that are present. This is everyday mindfulness, at home, at work, and everywhere in between.

Be Your Own Therapist

Any therapist knows that what helps a client get well is not a bucketload of techniques but the relationship between therapist and client. This relationship needs to be one of trust, compassion and attentiveness. These are the very qualities we need to heal our own lives. We are divided within. We have parts of our being rejecting other parts. A part of us tells us we are being lazy if we sit down and take a break. We have other parts saying that we need to take it easy and not keep so busy. Some voices are telling us we need to be more courageous and other voices are telling us to accept ourselves. We notice qualities in ourselves we admire and others we just want to keep hidden. When we banish aspects of ourselves in this way, we experience ourselves as divided and unhappy. We cannot be divided and happy. We are either whole and happy or divided and unhappy. Meditation brings into consciousness all those banished parts and lets them have their place.

Our ability to touch love and kindness
and be touched by them lies buried below our
own fears and hurts, below our greed and our hatreds,
below our desperate clinging to the illusion
that we are separate and alone.[5]

FROM 'WHEREVER YOU GO, THERE YOU ARE'
JON KABAT-ZINN

When we sit in meditation, and indeed in our daily life, we need to be like a good therapist – attentive, compassionate and trustworthy. We don't enter into meditation with ideas of changing ourselves, but of loving ourselves. We welcome everything there is and reject nothing. The Buddha wasn't happy because he rejected parts of himself, he was happy because there was nothing in him that wasn't worthy of honouring.

A divided mind causes tension and is the source of inner conflict and unhappiness. It wants to experience only certain aspects of life: the pleasant and acceptable. But life brings everything, the joy and the pain, and if we only want half of it we will suffer because of what we are running away from.

An undivided mind, a mind that is whole, turns away from nothing and accepts everything. It experiences life as it is right now, completely in each moment. That is why the Buddha was happy – he didn't try to control life, but surrendered completely to it and so was at peace. Whether it was pleasure or pain, he experienced it fully. That is the path of meditation – to experience life now and not be constantly distracted by dwelling endlessly on the past and the future.

*An undivided mind, a mind
that is whole, turns away from nothing
and accepts everything*

DANCE WITH THE DRAGON

◆

As a child, I once read a story about a princess who kisses a dragon and the dragon turns into a prince. It was only years later that I realized that the dragon was a metaphor for the scary emotions the princess tried to avoid; but by befriending the dragon she welcomed her other half – she became complete. Perhaps our own dragons are waiting for us to act with courage and compassion.

THE DISCIPLE ASKED THE MASTER to tell the students about the human condition, then settled down to hear what the master had to say. The master sat up, looked around the room, then said, 'Caught in thought.' This may not be a very elegant answer and probably not one we want to hear, but how true it is. Whenever we experience uncomfortable emotions, the mind asks, 'How can I get away from this?', 'How can I be free of this fear, sadness or anxiety?' You can't! Our attempts at getting away from negative emotions merely strengthen them. The problem isn't the negative emotions but how we view them and our resistance toward them.

What I normally suggest to people is to turn gently and compassionately toward experience, no matter what it is. Be aware of the stories the mind is running. When we turn toward emotions that we have habitually turned away from, the mind can become unsettled. It may give us reasons for not doing this, it may spill out dark scenarios about what might

happen if we stay here. If this happens, be gentle but firm. Don't overdo it – if it gets too much, then that is fine, we can accept the fact that we have had enough for the time being.

Healing the Wound

I remember an occasion in the early 1990s, when I had been meditating only a few months. I was sitting in meditation and felt a sensation in my stomach area. The immediate impulse was to stop and do something. However, I had committed myself to meditation and resolved to remain sitting. So I gently took my awareness to that area and it felt like a wound. As I stayed with it, I noticed it felt about the size of a small saucer. As I sat with it, an image came to me of a weeping wound. It felt like a lot of hurt from the past was right there in that wound. Intuitively, I knew that what I had to do was to be with it in a compassionate way. I didn't try to do anything to it – get rid of it, zap it with healing light, or even work out why it was like that. I just sat with it day after day. Some days it was strong and other days it was barely noticeable. After many months, I noticed that I was feeling lighter, as if I had put down a heavy load that I had been carrying for an age. At the same time, I realized that the 'wound' hadn't been around for a while. It became obvious to me that something had healed. This one experience gave me more trust in awareness than anything else has done. Awareness heals our lives if we have the courage to 'stay at home' with ourselves.

This is how we transform negative feelings and emotions, how we transform those dragons into princes (or princesses) – by compassionately experiencing them. Wisdom and compassion grow out of our experience of life. As we turn toward ourselves, we gradually become comfortable with what we previously found intolerable and our capacity to hold life increases. Your view of life may be that if you keep pain away, then you will be happy – but ask yourself whether this approach has ever really worked. To be truly happy in life, we need to experience the whole of life. It is then that the transformation takes place. We have learned the steps of the dance.

Never Turn Away

◆

All of us, to varying degrees, have aspects of ourselves that we either don't like, are ashamed of, or are afraid of. If you think you don't, then you are either very spiritually mature or you don't know yourself very well. Or perhaps you don't want to know yourself.

NORMALLY, WE KEEP THE PARTS OF OURSELVES we don't like well hidden from ourselves and others. However, they leak out in various ways. It may be covert behaviour, sneaky remarks, gossiping, or anger that we don't want others to see. We keep these hidden because we have a view of ourselves and these aspects don't fit in with that view. I had a view of myself as a generous person, and indeed there is that

◆

The most fundamental aggression to
ourselves, the most fundamental harm we can
do to ourselves, is to remain ignorant by not
having the courage and the respect to look
at ourselves honestly and gently.[6]

FROM 'WHEN THINGS FALL APART'
PEMA CHÖDRÖN

◆

aspect, but when I was on meditation retreats – and I was leading them – I noticed how obsessed I could become when queuing for the meals. I would stand there hoping that the guy in front wouldn't get the large piece of pie that was left, or worry that there wouldn't be enough porridge left for me if I wasn't at breakfast early. I realized that although I am capable of generosity, I am also capable of being greedy and obsessive. At this point, I began to recognize not just the aspects that I liked but also the parts that I didn't. I started to bring into consciousness all those banished energies/parts that I viewed as unacceptable because I was either uncomfortable with them or frightened of them.

This led to a very different way of practising mindfulness meditation. When I say 'practising mindfulness', I am talking about our sitting practice and everyday life.

I found that instead of trying to control my experience so that I could feel good, I would bring curiosity to it. I would

welcome the very parts I was previously running away from. This led me to face myself in a way I never had before, and it's been the best thing I have done.

Love & Accept Yourself

This is how I now teach mindfulness meditation. Instead of controlling and running from their experience, I encourage people to turn kindly toward whatever it is that is upsetting them or that they are afraid of. This is a way of bringing love and acceptance into meditation rather than control and judgement. This approach to mindfulness is a way of truly loving yourself, of saying to all those hurt parts, 'I am not abandoning you any longer. It may take me a while to accept you but I am going to do my best.' And our best is all we can do. It is not about heroic endeavours but more about the little ways in which we are willing to stay with uncomfortable sensations and feelings instead of zipping off to use the internet, phone a friend or eat more cheese. Sometimes, we may reach something that just feels too much right now, and that is accepted too. As well as curiosity, we need patience and compassion.

I am occasionally asked, 'Why do this?' Well, either you are drawn to wanting to heal your life or you are not – and if you are, I have found that mindfulness and compassion meditation when practised intelligently does work.

When I meditate nowadays, I rarely turn away from myself, no matter what is present. I know that I am a good person,

and I know that I am capable of some pretty nasty things. The difference now is that I am aware of them and mostly I don't act them out.

Love & Accept Others

One of the main benefits of healing in this way is that we become more comfortable with ourselves and other people. Once I stop demonizing parts of myself, I stop demonizing that very same behaviour/trait in others. Mindfulness is a path to liberation, compassion and happiness, a path worth taking whatever trials you may encounter on the way.

Forgiveness Practice

Sit down and bring to mind something about yourself you find difficult. It may be violent or sexual thoughts, maybe dishonesty or secrecy, it doesn't matter. Notice your reaction to this and how it makes you feel. Give it space, and breathe. Notice the thoughts about this, too. Stay with this for a few minutes, then just drop it into your heart. Don't be scientific about it, don't ask, 'Where's the heart?' The intention is enough. The heart always receives and forgives without judgement. If there is judgement, that is not the heart, so then drop the judging into the heart too. This is an act of compassion.

So I urge you never to turn away from your pain but to turn gently toward and even greet it. Treat it like a hurt child and give it space to feel as it wants to feel and to reveal itself to you. This is not analysis or trying to work out why we feel like this, but more like simply being with whatever is hurting. We tend to have a view that if we keep bad feelings out of awareness, we will be well. Not so. They stay around and often rebel in the form of negativity or illness. What we often fail to see is that if we have anything inside that feels sick, ill or uncomfortable, we can turn toward it and breathe. Let it be felt. This is the way it can release and transform into what it needs to. This is the way of compassion, and compassion to oneself is compassion to the whole of life.

THE MINDFUL BODY

It seems that the desire to be other than we are is very common, that most of us have something about ourselves we want to change. We may use the language 'transforming' or 'letting go', but what we're really saying is: 'How do I change myself?'

THE THEME OF HOW WE CHANGE has been of some interest to me since my wonderful days of living in the retreat centre. I have noticed that if I have difficult experiences, I can so easily use strategies that are not helpful. For example, if I find myself being unkind or angry with others or myself, I can

easily try too hard to be the opposite. Of course, there needs to be an element of restraint from acting unskilfully, but that in itself is not enough. If I simply attempt to block out and ignore how I am and try to be different, I am not actually dealing with the issue of how I am in the present. Other responses I may have are swinging between condemning myself and wishing to be different. If I follow the approach of trying to be different, I end up being a bit like an overstretched elastic band – sooner or later I will ping back to my old behaviour because I have not resolved the issue, I have merely been trying to avoid it.

If I find myself being unkind or angry, then instead of trying to be different I can decide to actually be with the experience of unkindness or anger – I can decide to be mindful of my present experience.

Noticing the Body

So what do I do to be mindful? I can feel the experience of anger, sadness, fear, anxiety or joy in the body. When I experience anger and similar emotions that I label negative, the body tends to contract. I can be mindful of what the contraction, the anger, feels like. I can even take away the label and turn and experience the energy afresh, without a label. Where in the body is it actually experienced? What does it feel like? Has it got a centre? Is it fixed or is it slowly changing as I watch it? I may find myself lost in thoughts about it all and

come to see how belief in thoughts actually generates the emotion, but when I notice this I can again bring mindfulness to my experience in the body.

After a while, I may notice something else. I may sense that beneath the anger is hurt or fear, which is what the anger was preventing me from experiencing. In all of this, there is no judgement about the anger as a bad thing – I already know that it can be destructive if there is not awareness of it. If I had tried to be different or to cultivate the opposite quality prematurely, I would not have gained insight into the nature of it. I would not have realized the changing-ness of the energy, I would not have seen that it was protecting a hurt feeling, and I would not have noticed that if I take away the label, it becomes much more interesting and less scary to be with. I may even notice that what I normally label 'anger' is frustrated assertiveness, which, if expressed, would ironically save me from a lot of anger. But if I am too quick to label/judge my experience, I never get to see this. If I can be mindful in this way, I actually strengthen the capacity of mindfulness. My ability to be aware in the midst of strong experiences increases. In a word, I become more AWAKE – which is the reason I practise.

After a while, I realize that instead of *trying* to be a kinder person, I actually *become* one by experiencing and being mindful of my unkindness or my anger. Through mindful experiencing of anger, over time the roots of it are dealt a mortal blow. I can now have deeper faith in the power of

mindfulness as the way to freedom. I also realize that mindfulness is much more than merely observing myself from somewhere in the head – but if mindfulness isn't just about that, then what is it? I find that mindfulness is somehow a sense of aware presence. It is having a sense of what is happening, here and now, rather than just noting it from somewhere inside the head.

Mindfulness is Wisdom

I come to see that mindfulness is wisdom; it is a compassionate space that allows joys and sorrows to be born and to die within it. It gives me faith to face myself and have the courage to turn toward experiences that I would previously have turned away from. It is a way of compassionately listening to myself, a way of listening to life through all the senses. And there is something else about mindfulness that I have come to see – that it is much more than all the above. It is a mystery.

Mindfulness allows me to follow the middle way of the Buddha. If I am mindful then I am less likely to fall into extremes. For example, if I am angry then I am more capable of not repressing it on the one hand and less likely just to express it unkindly on the other. I find the middle way here is to experience the energy of it in the body, to acknowledge its existence but not to allow myself to get caught up in the story about it, by getting lost in blaming either myself or other people or the world.

While my practice is primarily about mindfulness in the way I described above, it is completely at one with the development of generosity and compassion through my actions with other people.

As we have already seen, many people meditate with the aim of getting away from their experience. Sometimes it seems that to experience themselves is too much – so let's switch it all off! This is how I approached meditation for years. I could use the terms 'relaxing' or 'calming' as a euphemism for wanting to extinguish my experience. That is why, nowadays, I emphasize the *breath* and the *body* in meditation. To be aware of what the body feels like, to be aware of all its tensions and contractions, all the numb parts and all the open and alive parts. To be aware of whether the breath is natural or feels controlled, cramped or shallow. This is what I find helps lead to integration.

The End of a War

Over the years, there have been times where I have been quite uncomfortable with myself, often feeling like I was never quite good enough in some way. But in recent years, instead of trying to be different or to ignore those feelings, I have allowed myself to mindfully experience, with compassion. As a consequence, I am now more at ease, and those feelings are not the problem they used to be. Though, of course, there are still times when an emotion comes and takes me by surprise.

Through body awareness, I am able to release and integrate all those banished energies that I thought were unacceptable and that I had to keep at arm's length. Meditation, for me, has meant letting go of being at war with myself. This is what I share with people on courses – that it is OK to feel anything, it is OK to allow 'bad', negative thoughts to arise rather than trying to keep those thoughts hidden or condemning themselves for having them.

Here again, the analogy of melting ice is useful. If we have an ice cube, all we need do for it to dissolve is to put it in the heat and leave it. Our bodies are similar. Often our feelings can be 'frozen out' of awareness because they are painful to experience. If, though, we are willing to bring mindfulness to our bodily experience, to feel it just as it is and to 'listen' compassionately, it begins to soften. Just as the ice cube dissolves into its original nature, which is flowing water, so our bodies, too, soften and our feelings start to flow again.

Sense of Self

I often sit and ponder on the sense of self that I experience, and at one point the image of a clenched fist came to me. I experience my sense of self as a big contraction, just like this clenched fist. It has been like that for so long that it seems normal. It takes a lot of effort, a lot of mindfulness practice, to unclench myself. But what I have realized is that it takes more effort and energy to keep it all clenched, because it's

not the natural way to be – it is a protective strategy, based on an incorrect view that I am a separate and fixed self.

Reality seems too much, so it's safer to keep clenched and to keep myself from opening up and seeing things as they really are. It seems to me that seeing things as they are and opening up the clenched fist of selfhood are part of the same process. What I need to do is to look at my incorrect belief in a fixed self, and also unclench the bodily counterpart.

What happens if, in meditation, I sit and experience this clenched-ness, this contraction? It very slowly begins to reveal its secret. It begins to open, to soften; sometimes energy may be released, other times I can experience fear and agitation. Sometimes there is a resistance to being with this, other times there is much joy and satisfaction. Often I reflect on my belief about this fixed sense of self, which can again lead to the same experience. But throughout all this, I have faith in mindfulness.

It seems to me, then, that the body is a crucial area of spiritual practice. It helps me emotionally and psychologically and helps me spiritually, too. The question now arises – just what is the body?

Reality seems too much, so it's safer to keep clenched and to keep myself from opening up and seeing things as they really are

EXERCISE

THREE-STEP BREATHING SPACE

This is a portable meditation practice, which can be very useful for our everyday lives – especially when things get a bit hectic. You don't need to get into a special posture so this can be done in the office, the checkout queue or just about anywhere. Do it for 10 seconds or a few minutes – whatever you need.

STEP 1 **Acknowledging**

Acknowledge right now what is happening. How you feel and what thoughts are present. Just observe.

STEP 2 **Breath**

Take your attention to the breath – the breath can be an anchor so just experience it as it comes and goes.

STEP 3 **Body**

Expand awareness to include the whole body. Just feel how the body is – be interested.

And that is it. Its power is in its simplicity. You can do this several times a day and those around you won't even notice as you integrate it into your daily life.

UNTYING EMOTIONAL KNOTS

◆

We can see mindfulness practice in terms of 'untying the knots' – the knots we created yesterday, last week, last year, and the knots from childhood. The older the knot, the more difficult it is to untie. But untie it we can, if we know how.

UNTYING KNOTS IS BOTH SIMPLE *AND* DIFFICULT. The simplicity lies in the fact that all we need do is give the knot of energy some compassionate attention. The difficulty is that it's normally the last thing we want to do, because it means facing ourselves here and now.

Every time we get into negative states – blaming, condemnation, resentments, complaining, self-criticism, among numerous others – we tie a knot in our body, and it stays there until we learn how to untie it and let it go. It is the body that pays the price of all these knots. Over the course of our lives, can you imagine just how knotted the body can become?

It seems that, left to our usual way of being, we don't know how to let go of the knots that we tie every day – unlike animals. The other day, I watched two dogs growling and getting ready to fight. The adrenalin was coursing through them. Luckily, they parted without a fight; but what I noticed was that one of the dogs wagged its tail vigorously afterwards as a way of releasing the energy, then off it trotted with not a care, and all was well again.

It didn't seem to hold on to the event like we humans do. What do we do when we get upset with someone or something? We dwell on it. We tell ourselves the story over and over again. 'I'll get him', 'How could she say such a thing?' or 'I'll never get a job, I'm going to be poor for the rest of my life.' Stories, stories, stories, over and again. We find it difficult at first to let go of these stories but with practice it becomes increasingly easier.

Two Steps to Freedom

Noticing how we rerun the stories is the first step in becoming free of the knots. So when we are telling ourselves how bad life is or how horrible someone has been to us, we need to notice those thoughts. Notice the effect they have on our bodies. Then we step away from the stories and come back to the present moment, which includes the body. Simply come back to the body and the senses. Don't let yourself dwell on those dark thoughts – they are killing you and your life.

So that is how we stop creating more knots – by noticing when we are tying them. In time, you will find this easier and you will be more relaxed.

The second step is freeing ourselves of knots we have already tied. This is again done through awareness of the body. When sitting, bring your awareness into the body and feel it. You may notice parts that feel tense or tight, like a fist or a tight belt, but whatever it is, just feel it and be curious. By curious, I mean

EXERCISE

UNTYING EMOTIONAL KNOTS

Do this practice for 5 minutes to begin with as it can have powerful results, then build up to 15 or 20 minutes.

• Spend a few minutes establishing a connection with the body. Feel your feet, legs and hips, sensing into the belly and around the back. Move up the spine and feel around the shoulders … then around to the chest. Notice the arms and hands … then move up and feel the head.

• Now take your attention to your breath and feel the quality of the breath for a few minutes. Be curious. Notice anything that feels uncomfortable; mainly around the middle body – the belly, chest and throat – just feel around and see what you find. Perhaps you notice a holding in the belly, or a heaviness in the chest; perhaps the throat feels tight. It may be fuzzy and unclear, but you sense there is something there.

• Locate it in the body as best you can, and allow yourself to explore it. Perhaps it is a physical sensation or it may be more emotional.

• Be interested … give it space … feel around it … Notice its qualities … Is it hard or soft? Heavy or light? Sense what it feels like. If you get distracted by thoughts, notice them and return to the body.

• Stay with it as best you can for a few minutes, noticing its different qualities: tight, heavy, pinched, jumpy, scared or anxious.

• Now begin to expand awareness to include other areas of the body. The legs, the arms and hands, the head …

• Become aware of the breath as it comes and goes. For a few minutes, just be with the breath in this way. Relax with the breath; relax into any tensions you may find. Let any thoughts drift away like clouds …

• Have a sense of the room and any sounds. Now open your eyes and sit as you wish. Take a few moments to absorb the practice.

notice its different qualities. Is it hard or soft? What shape is it?
What texture? Is it heavy or light? Is there an emotion connected
to it? In my own experience, I often sense a holding in my belly,
or feel a clenching in my jaw.

And that is all you need to do. In time, you may notice
events from the past coming into awareness. This is the body
releasing the blocked energy. There may be tears, sadness,
or gladness and joy, but trust in the whole process and slowly
you will free yourself from the tyranny of carrying around the
burden of the past.

It's OK to Be Afraid

---

*A common question that arises from meditation practice is how to
deal with difficult emotions, such as fear. But the practice of mindfulness meditation asks that we don't do anything at all. If we are
experiencing fear, then leave it be, just as it is.*

WE ALLOW OURSELVES TO BECOME THE FEAR, become
intimate with the fear. We don't need judgements and
opinions about it; however, if we do judge, we simply notice
that. It's OK to be afraid, it's OK to be angry, it's OK to have
nasty thoughts about other people or ourselves. This is not an
excuse, however, for unkind behaviour.

No matter what is being experienced, we can move toward
it. Try touching the edges of it; take a walk around the other

side of it and see what it's like there. Keep exploring it and don't do anything intentionally to change it or get rid of it. I am not asking you to like it – that is different; but we can allow it a space to be.

Most of us can talk about our fear and anxiety very eloquently. To experience them is another matter; but when we turn toward emotions and sensations in this way, we are no longer their prisoner. Only through experiencing our fears can we stop being a victim to them.

Where We Fear to Tread

This is where most of us, to begin with, don't want to go. We know that somehow our usual small sense of self is going to be obliterated, and indeed it will be; and this in itself keeps us at a distance from fear. It can feel like death, and in a way it is – a small death of the little self. The way we see the world is going to change if we allow ourselves to be with what is right here and now.

When you practise in this simple and direct way, there comes a time when you realize that something has changed. You really have no idea how it happened or even that it was happening, but you know that it has. You know that you are more at ease with yourself and the world.

It is a radical acceptance of life as it is. We accept the unfolding of life moment after moment and cease fighting against it. We don't need a running commentary about what's

happening in our life, we just learn to experience it as it is. This is the end of the inner war, and peace will reveal its beautiful head at some unexpected point.

Our usual experience is that there is a 'me' and the part of 'me' with which we are present. For example, there is me and then there is my fear. As we practise in this way, however, this duality, this separation, eventually dissolves, leaving a spaciousness that we never imagined, and this spaciousness contains everything that arises and opposes nothing. This is the blessing of the Buddha.

A Fear of Fear

For many years, even into my early forties, I was very uncomfortable with fear. I was hard on myself because I thought I shouldn't be afraid at my age. I thought I should always be courageous and bold. I would tell myself to get my act together and to stop being a wimp, but still the fear persisted. What I needed to do was to stop analyzing and criticizing the fear and instead get to know it. I saw that thinking about the fear didn't help me to understand it or be at ease with it; what was needed was awareness of the experience of fear. So whenever I experienced fear, I would be mindful of falling into the trap of thinking I knew what it was. I would approach it without any ideas of what it was or was about. I would notice my heaving chest, the feeling of wanting to distract myself and get away from it. I would observe the

agitation in my belly area, but I would stay with it. What I noticed every time was that if I gave it space to be, it moved of its own accord. I would also quite naturally identify what it was about, but that was secondary. The main point is that I stopped fighting it. I ceased to separate a part of my mind from it and remained whole. It wasn't always pleasant but over time my response to fear gradually changed.

It wasn't that I was brave, but I *was* curious. Curiosity is what enabled me to see what fear was rather than what I feared it to be.

During this period of investigating fear, I realized something that came as a big surprise. I realized that I was never afraid of *people* but only fearful of my *own emotional response* to them. I saw that I was afraid of certain emotions that people sparked within me and I was afraid because I didn't know how to handle my own emotions. I am not, of course, talking here about people who might be physically dangerous, as it's perfectly healthy to be afraid then. But all of us can learn in our daily life to embrace our fears, experience our fears and move beyond them.

◆

Curiosity will conquer fear

even more than bravery will.

JAMES STEPHENS (1880–1950)
IRISH POET

◆

95

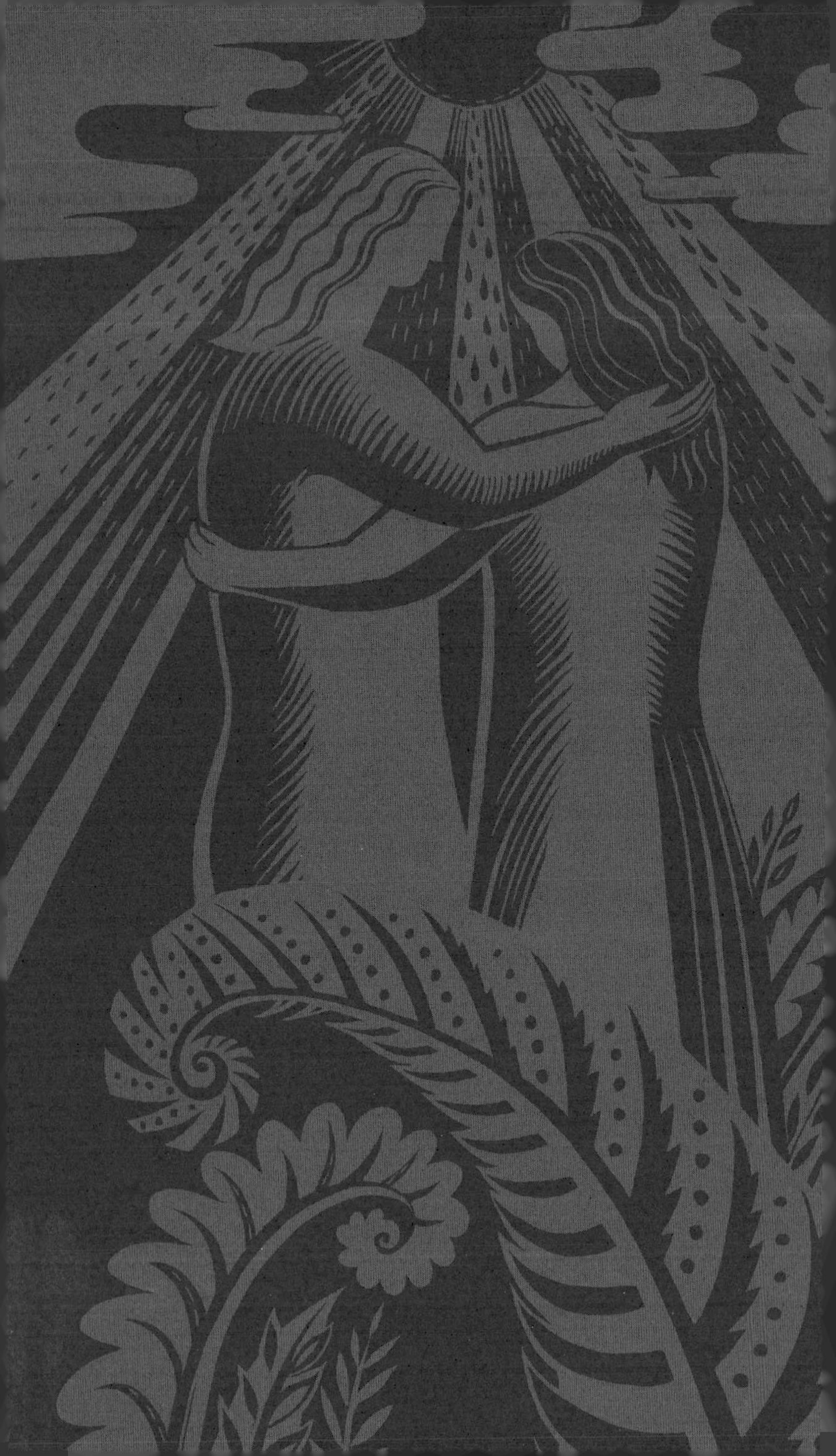

CHAPTER FOUR

WAKING UP
TO EACH MOMENT
OF YOUR LIFE

*Often in life we look for the special and
exciting. We don't want to be with the ordinary
everyday things like washing the dishes, vacuuming
the house or sending emails. Yet in Zen Buddhism, the
highest of practice lies not in experiencing the glories
or higher states of consciousness, not in sitting at the
side of the Buddha of golden light or experiencing
god-like bliss, but in stirring the porridge. There
is no glamour or glory in stirring porridge; it
is just about bringing alive the mundane
and simple aspects of life.*

STIRRING THE PORRIDGE

◆

We all have mundane everyday activities, but quite often we resist, which leads to tension and distress. Our mindfulness practice is about observing how we are with the everyday — walking up the stairs, tying our shoelaces, sending an email, eating a sandwich.

D O WE NOTICE HOW WE WANT to be doing something else? Do we observe when we are present with the activity we are engaged in? Being in the NOW is the buzz term nowadays, but do we know what it really means? It has very little to do with golden light and feeling cosmic bliss and everything to do with stirring the porridge.

I remember my days of training in Buddhism when on retreat. We always had periods of doing chores and I really didn't like it. I would curse and resist like hell. 'I don't want to do this sort of work.' But slowly the penny dropped and I came to see that everything, no matter how mudane, could be a practice in mindfulness.

Our practice when engaging in these activities is to notice when the thinking, dreaming mind takes us away from the here and now. We say a gentle but firm 'no', then we return to the activity at hand, *back to* the present moment. We don't need to judge ourselves for thinking about a million and one things, but simply notice and return to the body and the activity we're doing at the time.

Resisting the Present

However much we tell ourselves that we want to live in the present, and *should*, we don't. We see ourselves time and again off on some daydream or regretting some past action. It is good to know the consequences of indulging in certain kinds of thinking. Most of it may seem to be innocuous little daydreams but these distractions are the way ignorance maintains its hold over us. If the thoughts are charged with strong emotion, such as anger or revenge, we know that indulging these can lead to harmful behaviour. So instead we simply observe our emotions, observe our thoughts, and return to the present moment.

Being Present in the Midst of Pain

In times of happiness and pleasure, it is quite easy to be aware of the present. When we are happy, our self-image is much more fluid. Our mind is undivided and whole and we are at peace. However, when pain arrives it is quite a different thing and it doesn't really matter whether it's physical or psychological. We don't like this. The mind then becomes separated from experience and goes into conflict with the pain. It may use its usual strategies of trying to get rid of it, condemning it or even shutting down. It is only when we see clearly that these strategies don't work that we stop employing them.

EXERCISE

LENGTHENING THE OUT-BREATH

In this technique, we lengthen the out-breath by a second or two. This works because to lengthen the out-breath we need to give our attention to it – which means we must take our attention out of our thinking.

Just do this for a minute or two at the most. You can, though, do it many times a day – this is my personal favourite when I feel a little rushed. I find it really grounds me in the present moment, which feels very satisfying.

We stop trying to do something to the pain – we learn to accept it as part of life and we mature as a consequence.

Learning to come back to the present moment even in the midst of pain is what matures us as human beings. We are not being martyrs here, we are not looking for pain, but if it is there we stop pretending otherwise. There are two ways to suffer. Either we suffer with awareness and learn from it and let it season and mature us or we just resist by any method we can. Those methods may include over-drinking, over-work, keeping busy, running away from responsibilities. Blaming others is a very common way of not experiencing our own pain.

At Peace with Fear

When I first started practising Buddhism in the early 1990s, I had a lot of fear inside me. I used various strategies to get rid of it but none of them really worked. The fear was still there most of the time. I knew the *theory* of meeting fear and had read the books, but I didn't understand it until I had a dream while on a solitary meditation retreat. In the dream I had to go into a room in a house. As I approached the room, I realized there was a raging fire inside it. Of course, I did not want to enter and stood by the doorway, wondering what on earth to do. At that moment, a friend in the dream came by and pushed me into the room and I awoke with a start.

On waking, I knew instantly what the dream was telling me. It was showing me that I must enter into the fear – into the fire. Only by entering into it completely would I understand what fear is and be at peace with it. I realized that struggling against fear was a way of generating more fear. To be free from pain, we need to stop separating from it. When we do this time and again, we see that the only real possibility is to be with the pain just as we can be with pleasure. We need to learn the art of coming back to both the pleasant and the unpleasant in life. As one good teacher called it, this is the wisdom of no escape.

Stirring the porridge, then, is being with the whole of life without separating from it. It is allowing the joy to dance and the pain to sing. Our work is to create a big space in which it can all happen in its own beautiful way.

LIVING LIFE BACKWARDS

In Zen, there is a 'reverse' law. It means that when you try to float on water you sink, and when you try to sink you float. You need very little effort to stay afloat – simply fill your lungs with air. Easy, really. But hold your breath and you've lost it.

SIMILARLY, THERE IS A SAYING IN SUFISM: 'If you want to save your soul, then lose it.' But what does this have to do with mindfulness meditation? Well, we all find ourselves in a bit of a pickle about life. We find ourselves feeling afraid, confused and insecure. We may prefer to keep these 'beasts' at arm's length or, better still, just pretend they are not there. But they exist and will not simply go away because we want them to. Another way out of the pickle can be to pursue the opposite, so we embark on a mission to feel OK about life, to blot out the anxious, insecure tremble we feel. We may try to get a 'job for life', we may try to make sure that everyone we meet likes us and is nice to us. Or perhaps we make sure we have a pension, and surround ourselves with things or people who make us feel secure and good.

The Freedom of Uncertainty

Alternatively, we may tackle this problem by turning to philosophy or religion in order to make sense of this 'strange old world'. We may take on certain beliefs, maybe that there is life after death, or that this is it and when we die there is nothing. Both are beliefs, and can be a comfort to us; but to be utterly free we must move beyond mere beliefs into the realm of uncertainty, and this is where most of us don't want to go. The cause of insecurity is that our efforts go into finding security… and there is no security. This is it – there is no security; and to realize this is the *only* security.

We may try endlessly and ingeniously to make intellectual sense out of life. Thinking it through this way, thinking it through that way, but in the end hopefully we realize that thinking is limited. It is of a dimension that cannot comprehend reality, because reality includes thought, includes the rational, but cannot be contained and understood by it. It is like trying to tie down water with string – it is futile. We can tie ourselves in knots trying to figure it all out. For some of us, this intellectual pursuit becomes the reason for living, but in the end leaves us vulnerable and afraid.

So remember the reverse law. If you want to catch a deer, lay down in the grass and it may come out and kiss you on the nose. If you want enlightenment, don't chase it, just drop your opinions about it; and if you want security, then simply embrace insecurity.

LIVING IN THE PRESENT

◆

We all live in the present and can never leave it. Almost all our energy goes into trying to do just that, and it's all in vain. We try scheming, fantasizing, planning, remembering the past and anticipating the future; but all this only leaves us feeling anxious and exhausted.

So IF WE NEVER ACTUALLY LEAVE THE PRESENT MOMENT but our experience is that we rarely touch it, what is going on? What is happening is that this self, this little 'me' that seems to exist in our head, is in opposition to being present. This is why meditation can be difficult to begin with – the little me is threatened by the stillness and clarity of presence, so it keeps us busy with endless stories about how bad we are, about how we should be, how life should be, could be or used to be.

The little me is not real, it exists only as an idea in our heads, but it has been around so long that we take it to be who we are. This idea is behind all the heartache that we experience as human beings. This little me convinces us of its reality because it can look back and see its history – as a child, teenager and adult. But actually, if we pay attention, what we take as history is only thoughts appearing in this present moment. The little me, or the self image in our head, interprets these thoughts as proof that it has existed through time; but this is not how things really are.

Take a few moments to do this simple exercise: Try to look for the past and future without thinking about them. Do this over and over again until you see for yourself that the past and future are really only thoughts appearing now. You will soon come to realize that you cannot find the past or future without thinking about them. Without these thoughts, neither exists as a substantial entity, there is only the present moment.

This doesn't, of course, mean that we don't make practical preparations or plan for the future, but we do it without getting anxious about it. Life becomes much simpler and more joyful as a result.

People often ask how they can let go of the future and live in the present. The answer to this lies in letting go of our thoughts about the future and becoming familiar with our true nature, which is presence. To be at peace, we need to be able to think about the past and future without anxiety.

Scared of the Unknown

The little me creates the idea of a real future, then gets anxious about its own creation; this is one of the reasons why our minds are so busy. The little me is scared of the unknown and the future is unknown, so it scampers around anxiously trying to make sure everything is going to be OK. The more we believe ourselves to be the little me, the more we relate to it, and experience this little me panicking about the future, the less peace we will experience.

The little me cannot bear the fact that we are living in the now, in the present, because there is no room in the present for a separate and exclusive belief in this little me. Being present equals seeing clearly and experiencing the wholeness of all life. If we see clearly, we come to understand that this little terror in our heads is not truly who we are.

This is why meditation is so important – it allows us to see clearly. It is also why we resist it, and the one who resists it is, of course, the little me, because it knows that its reign as ruler will come to an end if there is enough awareness of how things really are.

The little me cuts us off from the rest of life, leaving us feeling that we need something to feel whole, when what we actually need is to see clearly who we really are.

Thinking & Presence

So how do we bring about our longed-for experience of living in the present? Our practice in meditation is to bring the chattering mind to rest in the body and the breath. Our work is to notice all the stories that the mind attempts to distract us with. As we sit in meditation, we observe the chatter, the blaming, the opinions and judgements about life. We simply label them – THINKING. We do this in everyday life, too. If we

Our practice in meditation is to bring the chattering mind to rest

are writing a letter, we notice the distracting thoughts and come back to the task at hand.

We gently bring the mind to rest in the body, the breath or whatever else is happening now. As we do this, we notice the spaciousness, the stillness, the silence that is inherent in our being.

We come to see that if the little me is the opposition to the present, our true nature is presence itself. We are born into presence and live from presence for a few years as children, until the fateful day when we are told we are not good enough and we must be better. We then start to mistrust the beauty and fulfilment of presence, which is our connection with the whole of life, and begin to conform to others' demands of how we need to be. In this conforming, we shrink up into our heads and begin to see the world out there as a threatening place to be either conquered or withdrawn from.

Sit Kindly

Please sit comfortably and be compassionate to yourself. Trust that your own inherent wisdom has brought you to this time of meditation and the contemplation of what is important in life. Meditation is not a space to get and attain something but is in itself an expression of your own wealth of beauty and fulfilment. Time, patience and kindness will allow meditation to blossom.

Be at Ease with Pain

To live in the present moment isn't thinking about the present moment. It isn't comparing the moment to a moment you had last December. That is comparison and comparison is thought – useful when necessary. To be alive in the present moment means there is nothing left out of the experience to compare. It is experiencing directly that you are life itself and not separate from it. There is not even a separate part of you thinking about the experience you are having. This is often a very pleasant experience, but with practice we learn to be with pain, too, in a similar way. We see that to be at ease with pain, the intelligent way is to surrender to it.

BEING NOBODY, GOING NOWHERE

◆

We are very good at noticing our failings and weaknesses so we strive to put them right, often by criticizing ourselves and trying to be different. This is briefly satisfying when we 'attain' our current goal; but then, because of the nature of desire for more, off we go again.

IT BECAME APPARENT TO ME a few years ago that being a person is pretty difficult, but trying to become a different or better person is even more difficult. I remember my life before I began practising mindfulness. I never felt good enough. I was constantly wishing to be a better person. I wanted to be a better public speaker and I wanted to be wise.

I wanted to be more compassionate and more generous and I wanted people to like me and to think I was a really cool person. I wanted to be clever like one friend and witty and handsome like another. I was in need of lots of approval from other people. It was exhausting.

Then, after years of criticizing and condemning myself and making myself miserable, I decided to try mindfulness meditation – and guess what! The same thing started happening. I then wanted people to see that I was very spiritual. I wanted people to see that I was calm and never got angry. I wanted to be a good student and to know all the different Buddhist concepts. I wanted everybody to think I was the best meditator in the whole universe. The list I had in my head of how I needed to be was endless.

Fortunately, however, I came to see these mind games for what they are. I realized that the desire to change is healthy and gets us to practise meditation, but we must become aware of this desire if we are not to be its victim for ever.

Looking for the Future

My view was that when I had succeeded in changing all the 'bad' parts of me into 'good' parts, then all would be well. I realized at some point that I was looking for wholeness and happiness only in the future.

I also saw that it's impossible to be happy in the future, because 'the future' is only a thought right here and now. The thought 'the

Trust

Trust is important. There is much fear and suspicion in our lives that we don't trust ourselves or anyone else very much. Sometimes we just live on the surface, just get by. I am not talking about trusting the ego, of course, there is no ego you can trust, mine included – but we can trust our awareness … I cannot make you do it, of course, but I can encourage you. The point is, if you don't trust awareness enough, you are always going to be thrown into doubt and self-disparagement. When I trust, it is in this attention. I trust in this ability to listen. The voice that says 'I can't stand it!' I don't trust that. But I trust my ability to listen to it and to know it for what it is. When some kind of condition or emotion comes up, or when there isn't anything at all, it is – 'like this'. Trust that! Trust just knowing whatever it is. If there is nothing, then nothing is 'like this'.[7]

FROM 'DON'T TAKE YOUR LIFE PERSONALLY'
AJAHN SUMEDHO

future' doesn't happen in the future and neither does anything else. It doesn't rain in the future, it rains now. We don't meet a friend for coffee in the future, we meet them now.

I was fortunate to come across teachings telling me that I was whole and complete right here and now and that I didn't need to change myself. Somewhere deep inside, this resonated with me. The teaching was asking me to observe the desire to be somebody, to be other than I am, and not to play the games the egoic mind was wanting me to.

So that is what I did. In meditation and in my daily life, I became aware of how the mind was constantly thinking, constantly analyzing, constantly trying to work it all out. It was wanting to think about what was wrong and what needed putting right, and of course IT knew exactly how to do it. I would notice (in meditation and everyday life) how I wanted to be seen as special and to be approved of, and how painful it was always wanting something from somebody else to feel OK. I could see that trying to be somebody didn't work, it didn't result in peacefulness of any sort, but then I fell into another trap – I would try to be the opposite. If trying to be special didn't work, I would try to be ordinary. I would then try to convince myself that not being special is OK. This was all going on in my own mind and was very confusing.

The attempt to be somebody is a posture of the ego, but so is the attempt to be nobody. With the practice of mindfulness we observe it all happening, without judgement or criticism.

When we are wanting, we are like the leaning tower of Pisa. We lean toward what we want, whether it's wanting things or wanting to be different. When we are caught up in wanting, we are not centred and we lose our balance.

Will we ever be perfect? Not a chance. But we can be compassionate and forgiving

However, by simply letting go of trying to change and being present with how things are with awareness and compassion, change starts to happen – not through brute effort, or by condemning ourselves (which actually just makes us feel more miserable), but by being a friend to ourselves as we are. Will we ever be perfect? Not a chance. But we can be compassionate and forgiving toward ourselves and others.

The Middle Way

We all experience ourselves as a person, as a self, separate from other selves. The problem is not that we experience ourselves in this way but that we take this as ultimately true. I am here and you are out there and that is the reality of life. If we experience ourselves as separate from life and others in this way, then we will see life as something we have to battle against, and often this includes other people. The self or 'I' is motivated to ensure its own survival and God help anybody or anything that gets in its way. It is motivated by fear and in some cases can resort to atrocious things to ensure it gets what it wants. The self or 'I' is always trying to achieve something or get somewhere. It is restless and is threatened by the stillness of meditation.

This tendency to try to be somebody or get somewhere is the opposite of what we do in mindfulness. When sitting in meditation, our intention is to observe all the tendencies to change, to plan, to scheme. We notice all the strategies the mind uses to entice us away from the moment. We notice when we are 'leaning' toward something. It may be a desire to have something – a holiday or a shopping trip. It may be a regret about something that's happened, and we acknowledge that and return to the moment. Our 'leaning' may simply be wanting to be more present in meditation and that too can be observed and let go.

The path of mindfulness is often referred to as the middle way. It is the middle way between suppression and indulgence. On the one hand, we are not suppressing all the desires and fears that arise in meditation. On the other, we don't allow ourselves to be dragged along by their energy. If we find ourselves in the midst of an emotional storm, we unhook ourselves from the thinking and return to our breath.

The Freedom of Being Nobody

To be truly nobody is the greatest freedom we will encounter. So long as we are caught in the idea that we need to be somebody

other than we are, then happiness will elude us. On the other hand, if we believe that we can escape the unpleasantness, the fear and horror of what life brings, freedom will remain beyond our grasp. This is called the wisdom of no escape. That there is no escape sounds rather horrific – after all, if we are afraid, we want to be free of the fear. But we are only stuck with fear when we try to escape it, because we make an enemy out of it. Instead of trying to escape from it, we leave it alone and let it take nature's way, which is to move on in its own good time. If we take away the label of fear and allow ourselves to experience the moment afresh, it moves freely into something else. It no longer lodges itself because it has nowhere to lodge, because there is nobody there resisting it.

Observing Yourself Without Judgement

Notice during the day when you want to be approved of. There is no need for judgement or criticism; just simply notice. Observe the need to be liked, observe when you nod in agreement with somebody when actually you don't really agree. Observe when you want to be noticed or not noticed, depending on circumstances.

Do all this without judgement or the need to change anything. Embrace everything about yourself and become your own best friend.

I WANT, I WANT, I WANT

◆

We all want something from life. It's the human condition to be constantly wanting. But we're like thirsty men in the desert breaking open stones for water — it's just not there. It is the same with our attempts at getting happiness. It doesn't exist in the places we look.

WHERE DO WE LOOK? We look to relationships to quench our thirst for happiness, but they just don't deliver. We look to work, holidays, hobbies and trying to change the world. None of these bring the happiness we want. I am not saying we shouldn't pursue these, I am saying they will not bring absolute happiness. They bring pleasure and times of joy and comfort, but we want more, we want absolute happiness.

There is desire for wholeness, unconditional happiness, true joy, and the heart's release, whatever you want to call it. But because we are confused about what is really good for us, we translate this into meaning we need things, reputation, status, money and relationships. The plight of man can be said to be not knowing what truly makes us happy and killing ourselves trying to get it.

Running after reputation and so on is running after the promise that is never kept. Look at your own experience to verify this. How much does the mind promise? How often is it trying to fix life, or to work out what it needs to feel secure, only to move on to the next thing even if we do manage to get it?

Never Satisfied

Desire is never-ending and will never be satisfied, because desire's purpose is to desire. Once a particular desire has been satisfied, there may be a fleeting moment of happiness but then it's off again in search of more. How many times have we wanted approval from somebody? If we don't get it it's not satisfying and if we do get it it's still not satisfying, because five minutes later we want it again.

We have a belief that something, somewhere will make us happy, we have a belief that there will be a time and a place where we will find complete satisfaction. This is true, there is something that can bring absolute happiness; but this something isn't a person, a good or bad reputation, a career, or a solid gold pension. The only thing that can bring ultimate happiness is to know ourselves deeply and to see that all our views about getting satisfaction from the world are flawed. This is why disappointment is our guide on the spiritual path. Again and again we are disappointed about life. Again and again we see that the promise is not kept. So we eventually let go of hoping, and in letting go of hope, we let go of expectation and finally arrive at the place and time where happiness resides, here and now.

Desiring happiness or fulfilment is like an ache. It's a heartache that doesn't go away until it is heeded, and that ache is our guide. Our hearts yearn for freedom from the desire that keeps them desiring.

Anxiety About the Future

◆

Anxiety can be very useful as a prompt when you need to get some-
thing done — your tax return, for example. However, much of our
anxiety is created by ruminating about the future and what may or
may not happen. We could say we suffer from too much future.

WHEN I WAS LEADING A RETREAT ONCE, somebody very
honestly said, 'I am always anxious about the future
and I don't want to get old and die in this state.' Ironically, you
could argue that this statement itself is about future anxiety,
but I didn't say that.

Anxiety about a future implies that there is one. If we take
a good look at what the future is, we cannot find it. When we
look for the future, we find only thoughts about it; the future
itself never amounts to anything more than a thought or an
image. It's the same with the past, which we can so often
hanker after or regret. The past is nothing more than a thought
when we look for it. So it's not anxiety about the future that
is the problem, but the belief in the thought that arises here
and now, which is telling a story about a future we don't have.
If we look for any event in the past or future, all we find are
thoughts about the event. It does not mean it didn't happen
or won't happen, but the event itself can only be viewed now
in the realm of thought. We can still learn from it or prepare
for it, but if we see clearly enough that right now it is only

thought, then we won't get lost in anxiety or regret. This is not just playing with words because if you see this – and I urge you to do it – then it has radical consequences.

Intelligent Planning

We spend our time worrying because we attempt to protect ourselves from getting hurt and having problems. It's a way of trying to control events that we don't even know are going to happen. Now this doesn't mean that when we don't take our thoughts about the future seriously we become stupid and drop all responsibility; just the opposite. We can then discern the thoughts that are meaningful from those that are not. For example, we may plan which school to send our children to; that is intelligent planning for the future. What isn't intelligent is if it takes over our mind space and we get anxious about the whole affair; it has then got out of hand. Thoughts are like tools – we use them when necessary, then let them go. Through mindfulness, we become skilled at using thoughts then letting them go.

What I suggested to the questioner on the meditation day was to see that thoughts arise and pass away. When we do this for some time, we create space in the mind, which allows intuitive awareness to function. This is a 'function' of humans that is normally not noticed because we don't trust in it. What we trust in are the thoughts that stampede through our heads and often drive us to despair. I asked her to label her thoughts as just 'thinking', then return to her body, her breath, the present moment. The present moment includes thoughts but doesn't take a stand against them or cling to them like flies to flypaper. In the present moment, when we are not preoccupied with the streams of thoughts, we learn to trust in something else; that something else is our true home, our natural intelligence.

What's the Point?

From our own personal viewpoint, we want to think that there is a point to life. We want to think that there is a deeper meaning to getting up in the morning, going to work, waiting in traffic, getting angry and coming home. Surely, we think, there must be a point to all this.

WE HOPE THERE IS SOME MEANING in getting washed… again, in loving our partner (or not), zipping up our flies, getting frustrated by political correctness. We spend most of our lives engaged in mundane activities like eating a cheese sandwich, washing our hands, listening to more 'bad' news, brushing dandruff from our shoulders, talking to ourselves, going to bed and doing it all again. These daily activities, which are actually the activities that make up our lives, can seem pointless if we ponder too long on them… Best to keep ourselves busy, then!

They seem pointless because we are out of touch with ourselves or, put another way, they seem pointless because we feel separate from life. Our usual experience of ourselves is that there is me here and you and the world out there... We can feel separate, cut off and alone.

I'd Be OK If...

From the personal viewpoint, there is always something that needs to change or not change, happen or not happen in order for us to be OK. We have opinions and judgements about almost everything that's happening around us and these opinions are mostly about how an event will affect us. We have judgements like, this shouldn't be happening, that should be happening, life needs to be like THIS! It is all self-referential, from the viewpoint of the little me inside our own heads. But from the viewpoint of life itself, everything is just as it needs to be. So can you see the gap where suffering arises?

Meditation is about investigating this little me, this sense of self that we all have and which is the root cause of individual and global suffering. We all believe that if life goes right for us then we will be happy. The Jews and Arabs each think that if the other didn't exist, they would be OK. They wouldn't. The hatred is in their own hearts. You may think that if your boss only liked you more, or would get run over by a bus, then you would be OK – you wouldn't. You would still have that same pattern within you. This pattern is ready to be activated next time you meet somebody similar; and life will bring that person, because until we deal with it, we unconsciously seek out these challenges to learn from them.

Get to Know Your Own Life

Meditation is about finding out who we are here and now in our everyday life, not about floating off into some imaginary pink cloud. As we bring awareness to our lives, we notice that this sense of self, which is always needing something, is actually a mental construct that exists only in our heads and is maintained by our believed thoughts. It is the belief in this self that makes us feel separate from life and so we endeavour desperately to find meaning in it as compensation.

While we are trying to find meaning to life, we miss life. We turn from the wonder of life in all its glory to worry about life because it's not going as we expect it to; we're encountering too much fear, too much anxiety, and we're not getting what we really want. We try desperately to get life to give us meaning and happiness, when actually our life can be an expression of meaning, an expression of our happiness.

So get to know your own mind and emotional life and you will then notice changes in your life. Be compassionate, always compassionate to yourself, no matter what. Observe yourself in your daily activities and exchanges with other people especially. Observe when you want to be approved of or noticed. Observe when you tell a lie to get out of some-

thing. Notice how you say yes to somebody when actually you mean no. Observe your fears and desires without any judgement. As we notice this little me, this self in action, it will eventually lose its power to control our life and the question about the meaning of life won't even be a question any more. In its place will be freedom and happiness.

THE TYRANNY OF TIME

◆

What is this thing called time? We organize our lives around it, and it seems so real. But time isn't a thing, it does not exist as an entity in its own right. It is simply an idea in our head. A useful idea, but only that.

TIME IS A CONCEPT WE ALL SHARE so we can live together in an organized and efficient way. If we didn't have the concept of time, there would be complete chaos – the trains would be late and that wouldn't do!

Our relationship to the concept of time is what is important. In today's busy world, time can seem like a burden, but it isn't. If something doesn't exist, it cannot be a burden. The burden we experience is to do with our own incessantly busy minds. *People often say that there is not enough time in the day – but what they really mean is there are too many thoughts.* We have so many thoughts stampeding through our minds, telling us we need to do more activities, and get more things done in a day, a week, a lifetime. We are convinced that this second we are living was preceded by billions of other seconds and has billions of other seconds following it. We spend a lot of our time thinking about the billions of seconds still to come and trying to fill them in the most productive way possible.

Anticipating the Future

However, if we take a closer look at what we think time is, what we find are thoughts. If we think about the past, all we experience are thoughts, images, memories and feelings, which are happening now; likewise with the future. I often sit in meditation and intentionally look for the future. I am convinced it exists, but when I look for it, all I find are thoughts – which are happening now. What I realize is that nothing happens in the past, nothing happens in the future, because they don't actually exist, except as thoughts. If I think of a time when I was twelve, what I have are thoughts happening now, which create a certain mood now. It is the same with the future. A lot of my anxiety is because the future is uncertain, which I find uncomfortable. I want to know what is going to happen and that my loved ones and I will be well.

This belief in billions of seconds ahead of me, which I call the rest of my life, keeps me from living my life now, which is the only reality there is. At the moment of writing this, my partner and I are in the process of buying a new house. There are so many uncertainties around this, which can so easily

cause distress. However, when I look at the distress, the anxiety, about how things may go wrong over the next few months, what I find are thoughts and bodily sensations that are happening right here and now, which can make my life a misery if I let them. Yes, I have to think about what needs doing to make the house purchase happen and go well. I know that the time will arrive when we either sign the contract or it all goes belly up. But it is not happening in the future because there is no such thing other than a concept, and ruminating can only destroy my well-being.

A Limitless Container for Life

People often say to me that the past does exist and we need to learn from it. I agree we need to learn from mistakes, but to say that the past exists is not actually seeing things as they are. I ask them to show the past to me. I ask them to look for it and to tell me what they find. Nobody yet has been able to find anything other than thoughts and images about the past. I am not saying you were never twelve years old. What I am saying is that being twelve years old is only a thought presently. When you were twelve years old, being forty-eight was only a thought and being twelve only existed now. The now is also just a concept, because if there is nothing outside it, does it really exist as a separate entity?

I see the now as really the limitless container for life, all the events of life. This container holds all the changes and measurements we ascribe to time, as if it were a thing in itself. If we stop and pay attention, if we look, listen and feel right now, we come to see that all experience is directly experienced right now. After that immediate experience, we may

If we look, listen and feel right now, we come to see that all experience is directly experienced right now

have thoughts about it, which may then give rise to memories (more thoughts), which seem to suggest that there was an experience at another time – but that thought, any thought, any experience can only happen now.

I am not advocating never using the labels of past, future and now. I am encouraging you to know in your own hearts and minds what they really mean and to free yourselves from the tyranny of time.

Stepping Out of Clock Time

When we meditate, we have the opportunity to step out of clock time. There is no past or future in the hum of the refrigerator or the sound of a passing car. There is no past or future in the bodily sensations or the feel of the breath coming and going. If we enter directly our present experience and leave thought alone, we are left with pure experiencing without any notion of time. This experience enables us to see that time is a useful concept but that is all.

It seems that the power of memories and expectation is such that for most of us, the past and future are not *as* real, but *more* real than the present. It seems we cannot be satisfied unless the past is somehow miraculously cleared up and the future is brimming with promise. With this, though, we are dead to the wonder of this moment, because we are hypnotized by our thoughts about what was and what will be.

Most of our unhappiness seems to stem from dwelling on the bad things of the past and the possible bad events of the future. It's similar with happiness. It's as if most of our happiness is derived from thinking about good times of the past and pleasant expectations of the future. When those experiences arrive – if they arrive – we will only be dimly aware of them because we will be anticipating the next good thing.

Be Patient

This is where mindfulness can be very helpful, but we need to be patient. Mindfulness is a mirror – it shows us what is happening right now. It is not about changing what is happening but knowing what is happening. A mirror doesn't change anything but lets us see what is here. As we sit, we notice again and again the tendency to drift into a thought-made world. As we sit, we acknowledge these thoughts simply and with compassion. We let go and return once more to the breath or our bodily sensations. This is the way to a life of presence, kindness and quiet joy.

Looking for the Future

Sit down and be quiet for a few minutes. Now find the future without thinking about it or picturing it in any way. Search for it in your direct experience. If you look intimately enough, what you find is the present. Have another look. Does the future exist in the call of a bird, the feeling of cold feet, the smell of incense or toast?

The future does not exist anywhere except as thoughts in our heads. It is a useful concept but we take it to be real. It is the same with the past – we can learn from it but it does not exist except as a concept. Nothing exists outside of now, because now is the container for everything. It is similar to space – it contains all that is, even the anxious thoughts about the future.

THE ABC OF PRACTICE

◆

In the course of my work, I have tried in many ways to explain what happens when we practise mindfulness regularly. My most recent innovation, the ABC of Practice, seems to offer a healthy perspective on how to approach it.

THE STUDENTS ARE GATHERED in the meditation hall listening to the meditation teacher, when the teacher asks for questions. A student stands up and asks, 'Can you tell us the secret of life?' The master nods in agreement and sits himself down and looks around the room. The room is silent in anticipation and some students are even holding their breath, waiting for the wise words.

The master then sits up and says, 'The secret of life is knowing the difference between the contents and the container.' The students sigh, all rather disappointed at his response.

But what does this mean? If the master says this is the secret of life, perhaps there is something there for us to explore.

Container & Contents

Imagine we have a small glass almost full to the brim with water. Here we have the contents (water) and the container (the glass). If the glass is shaken or stirred, the water spills out because it is already nearly overflowing. So what is needed? A bigger container.

The water represents our thoughts, feelings / emotions and sensations – our internal experience. If the water represents our internal experience (the contents), then the glass represents our container – but what would this be? At this point, people often say the container is the body, which is partly true. The container, though, is really awareness, or we could say it is perspective.

Most people come to mindfulness practice thinking they are going to change the contents – unpleasant feelings and negative thoughts into pleasant feelings and positive thoughts. This does happen to some degree, but this is not what mindfulness is really about.

A Bigger Container

Imagine we put the same amount of water into a container two or three times the size and shake it in the same way. The water moves but it does not spill. This is, of course, because it is in a bigger container – there is more room. Mindfulness, then, is creating a bigger container. We still have all the same emotions and thoughts, though they do tend to become more benign and positive, but what really happens is that we create a bigger container – we increase our awareness of our emotions and thoughts. We can contain them. We no longer get so easily upset, just as the water does not so easily spill out.

Another way of looking at it is that we gain a greater perspective on ourselves and our reactions. Instead of taking our

emotions and thoughts very seriously, we begin to be able to be more at ease with them.

This is an organic process. A bigger container is not something we can *will* into being. It happens naturally over time, with regular practice. What upsets us now will not have such a dramatic effect in six months' time if we practise well. As we practise and are willing to be with ourselves rather than running away, we create this bigger container, which brings with it a peacefulness. It is peaceful because we are no longer pulled around by our thoughts and emotions.

The ABC

As you may have guessed, the ABC of Practice is A Bigger Container. The master pointed to this because through regular good practice we cease to identify so much with our thoughts and emotions. We don't take them all so personally. We come to see that we don't have to believe all our thoughts, we don't have to act on or fight against our feelings, because whatever arises soon passes if we don't interfere. It is a means of letting go into the natural way of things. Sounds arise and pass away, a bird in the sky appears then passes away, a plant or a tree arises then passes away – albeit generally more slowly than a sound. The point is that everything passes away and it is the same with our

Whatever arises soon passes if we don't interfere

thoughts and emotions if we allow them to take their own course. They flavour our experience for a while then pass on.

So developing a bigger container changes our relationship to our internal world and, I might add, changes our relationship to the external world, too – we might just be a little easier to live with.

What We Feel, We Heal

A woman who attended one of my courses was suffering with 'knots' in her stomach. She had researched the benefits of mindfulness and assumed this practice would help her banish the knots – her 'bad' feelings – once and for all, and change her experience from unpleasant to pleasant. After a few weeks, she told me that mindfulness was not working for her. I suggested that her mindfulness practice for that week should be to say 'hello' to any uncomfortable feelings and then do her best to move toward them and feel them: 'What we feel, we heal.'

These feelings did not suddenly vanish into thin air; the woman had to allow them into awareness so they could pass on. However, for feelings to pass on we need to change our relationship from one of conflict and resistance to one of friendliness and compassion. We do this by turning toward them and experiencing them as they are.

MINDFULNESS OF SELF & WORLD

◆

The reason our planet is on the edge of disaster is that most of us are self-centred. It's the way we are wired. To truly care for our world, we must move from a self-centred to a life-centred mode of existence, and this is what mindfulness is all about.

BEING SELF-CENTRED, we are caught up with our own desires, our own views and our own opinions. In this mode, our first priority is to satisfy our own neurotic desires (not natural desires, like food and friendship, etc) and to have our deeply held views proved right. We can easily tell if we are living from the self-centred mode – if somebody criticizes us and we feel hurt or hateful, we are living from the self-centred mode. In the life-centred mode, we can intuitively consider what has been said and respond in a way that is considered and more thoughtful. In the self-centred mode, we feel separate from life. It feels like we are here and life is out there happening to us. Feeling separate from life is really the essence of the self-centred mode of being.

The vast majority of us live in this self-centred mode of being. We may like to think we don't, but if we take a good honest look at what is going on inside, we will be in for a big surprise. The person living in the self-centred mode will have a headful of thoughts, because the self-centred person obsessively thinks about themselves and life, even though they may not realize it. The first priority of living in the self-centred mode is – ourselves. We may find ourselves thinking about our problems most of the day. We may notice how anxious we are about what the future holds. Living in the self-centred mode is hard because we are resisting the flow of life. It is an unnatural life. It is a life of tension and dis-ease because we are constantly on the alert for anything that can hurt us, which includes our reputation and status, among other things. Our energy in living in the self-centred mode goes into having people like us and/or not like us, depending on what will make us feel most comfortable. We seek comfort above all else.

A Life-Centred Mode

To live from a life-centred mode of being is very different, though it can look the same from the outside. Our motivations are not about satisfying our own needs and not about proving anything to ourselves or others in any way. When living from the life-centred mode, we don't care whether

> Mindfulness is about love and loving life.
> When you cultivate this love, it gives you
> clarity and compassion for life, and your
> actions happen in accordance with that.[8]
>
> JON KABAT-ZINN

Living in the life-centred mode, we don't feel separate from life, we are life

people like us or not. We are certainly not cold to others, but what they think of us is not really important. Our actions are motivated by what is best for all concerned in any given situation, and this concern for all concerned is compassion. This is not about being a martyr and sacrificing ourselves on the altar of doing good. Living in the life-centred mode, we don't feel separate from life, we *are* life. We don't need to obsessively think about life and how to make it work, we live in the moment and have a deep trust in the goodness of life, in our own deep goodness. In this mode, we find the jewel at the heart of the ice – natural happiness, love and a deep gratitude to our beautiful Earth.

So how do we move from being self-centred to being life-centred? This is what mindfulness meditation is all about. Through meditation, we come to see all the attitudes, beliefs and opinions that separate us from each other and life itself. These views, held strongly, are what lead to conflict and war. We come to realize that trying to fulfil our insatiable appetites is contributing to the problems in our world. One of the greatest wrong views we hold is that we are separate from life, separate from our world. This is the view that is doing damage to our planet. Through mindfulness, we come to see that this view is simply that – a view we have inherited through life, and is simply untrue.

We Are One

As we practise mindfulness and compassion meditation, we dissolve this feeling of separation and open ourselves to the wonder of life and our innate interconnectedness to all things and all beings. We see deeply that when we hurt another or our world, we are hurting ourselves.

When we live from the life-centred mode, we are living a natural life. We flow with the natural way of things. We know deeply that life is uncertain, impermanent and unpredictable. We have come face to face with these facts in our meditation and are at ease with them. In this life-centred mode, there is more energy available to us for following our calling. This is because we are not battling against the natural flow of life; we have surrendered our desires to the greater good, for the welfare of ourselves and of every living being on our precious planet.

Mindfulness and compassion are what our planet needs – not more idealism, but moment-to-moment mindfulness and a trust in the goodness that lies within us all.

ENDNOTES

1. *Wherever You Go, There You Are: Mindfulness Meditation in Everyday Life*, Jon Kabat-Zinn (Piatkus Books, London, 2004).

2. 'Wandering mind not a happy mind', November 11, 2010, *Hazard Gazette* online, www.news.harvard.edu/gazette/story/2010/11/wandering-mind-not-a-happy-mind/

3. *The Prophet*, Kahlil Gibran (Aziloth Books, London, 2011).

4. *Nothing Special: Living Zen*, Charlotte Joko Beck with Steve Smith (Harper-SanFrancisco, 1995).

5. *Wherever You Go, There You Are: Mindfulness Meditation in Everyday Life*, Jon Kabat-Zinn (Piatkus Books, London, 2004).

6. *When Things Fall Apart: Heart Advice for Difficult Times*, Pema Chödrön (Shambhala Publications, Boston, 1997).

7. *Don't Take Your Life Personally*, Ajahn Sumedho (Buddhist Publishing Group, Totnes, 2010).

8. 'Mindfulness in the Modern World: An Interview with Jon Kabat-Zinn', February 24, 2012, *Omega* online, www.eomega.org/learning-paths/body-mind-amp-spirit-meditation-mindfulness-health-amp-healing/mindfulness-in-the

FURTHER READING

◆

Happiness and How It Happens: Finding Contentment Through Mindfulness, The Happy Buddha (Ivy Press, Lewes, 2011).

Everyday Zen: Love and Work, Charlotte Joko Beck (Thorsons, London, 1997).

Nothing Special: Living Zen, Charlotte Joko Beck with Steve Smith (HarperSanFrancisco, 1995).

Wherever You Go, There You Are: Mindfulness Meditation in Everyday Life, Jon Kabat-Zinn (Piatkus Books, London, 2004).

Living With Awareness: A Guide to the Satipatthana Sutta, Sangharakshita (Windhorse Publications, Cambridge, 2003).

Don't Take Your Life Personally, Ajahn Sumedho (Buddhist Publishing Group, Totnes, 2010).

INDEX

THE MINDFULNESS SERIES

Mindfulness & the Art of Drawing
Wendy Ann Greenhalgh

Zen & the Path of Mindful Parenting
Clea Danaan

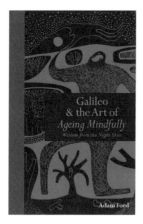

Galileo & the Art of Ageing Mindfully
Adam Ford

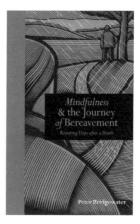

Mindfulness & the Journey of Bereavement
Peter Bridgewater

Mindfulness & the Natural World
Claire Thompson

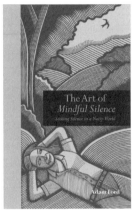

The Art of Mindful Silence
Adam Ford

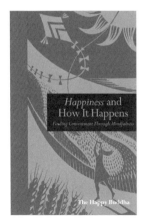

Happiness and How It Happens
The Happy Buddha

Mindfulness at Work
Maria Arpa

Mindfulness for Black Dogs & Blue Days
Richard Gilpin

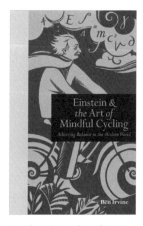

Einstein & the Art of Mindful Cycling
Ben Irvine

Mindfulness & the Art of Managing Anger
Mike Fisher

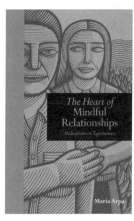

The Heart of Mindful Relationships
Maria Arpa

The Art of Mindful Baking
Julia Ponsonby

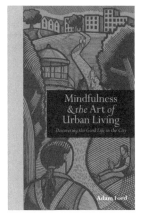

Mindfulness & the Art of Urban Living
Adam Ford

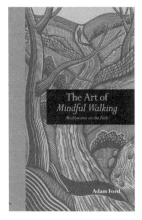

The Art of Mindful Walking
Adam Ford

Further Titles:

The Art of Mindful Gardening
Ark Redwood

Meditation & the Art of Beekeeping
Mark Magill

Zen & the Art of Raising Chickens
Clea Danaan

DEDICATION

For my teacher, Sangharakshita

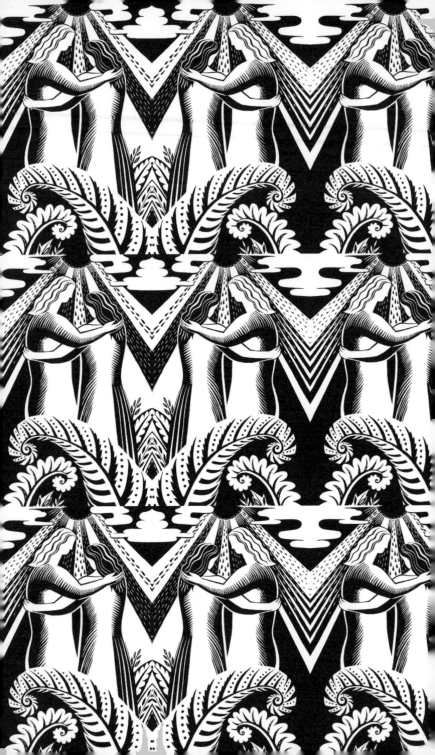